Playdate Publishing

PLAYDATE

~ with ~

Little Rock

CREATIVE ADVENTURES
FOR UNFORGETTABLE
FAMILY FUN

Emily Benton Ryan

Playdate with Little Rock

by Emily Benton Ryan

Playdate Publishing is an imprint of Sharp End Publishing LLC

Published and distributed by
Sharp End Publishing, LLC
PO Box 1613
Boulder, CO 80306
t. 303.444.2698   www.playdatepublishing.com

Playdate
Publishing

ISBN: 978-1-892540-77-5
Library of Congress Control Number: 2014935052

Cover Design: Concept by Russ Gray
Book Original Design: Sarah Durkee

Front Cover photo credits, clockwise from upper left corner:
Greek Food Festival, photo courtesy of Annunciation Greek Orthodox Church; Wonder Place, photo courtesy of Wonder Place; Mt Magazine, photo courtesy of Mt Magazine; Historic Arkansas Museum, photo courtesy of Historic Arkansas Museum; Blanchard Springs, photo courtesy of Blanchard Springs; Ozark Folk Center, photo courtesy of Arkansas State Parks; Wye Mountain, photo courtesy of Emily Ryan; Magic Springs, photo courtesy of Magic Springs; Magic Springs, photo courtesy of Magic Springs; Bobrooks Farm, photo courtesy of Evie Scherrey

Back Cover photo credits:
Little Rock Zoo, photo courtesy of Little Rock Zoo; Museum of Discovery, courtesy of Museum of Discovery; Two Rivers Bridge, photo courtesy of Todd Mikel Smith

Opening page photo credit:
Wonder Place, photo courtesy of Wonder Place

Photo credits are found in Photo Credits Index, pages 108 and 109. All unlabeled photos are taken by Emily Ryan or are a part of the Emily Ryan collection.

WARNING: You accept all risks associated with your use of this book and the information provided herein. You agree and understand that the information provided herein may not be accurate or complete. This book is intended to give outing suggestions for families. The author and publisher assume no responsibility for the condition of the site or damage to the site which may result in harm. Sites may not be appropriate for your child.

Acknowledgements

Dedication

To my parents, Beth and Bill Benton, for teaching me to be an adventurer

To Scott, for always believing in me and encouraging me

To my children, with all my heart, "I love you right up to the moon—and back"

Quotation

"Oh, the places you'll go! There is fun to be done!" -Dr. Seuss

Chapters at a Glance

1 Museums & More   11

2 Theater & Dance   25

3 Indoor Play Spaces   31

4 Reading is FUNdamental   47

Table of Contents

Maps of Site Locations

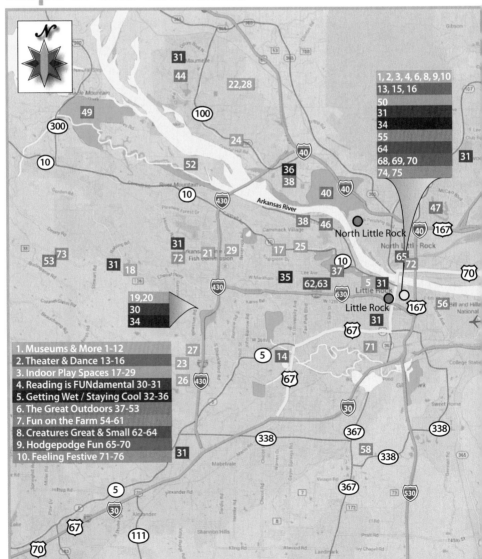

1. Museums & More 1-12
2. Theater & Dance 13-16
3. Indoor Play Spaces 17-29
4. Reading is FUNdamental 30-31
5. Getting Wet / Staying Cool 32-36
6. The Great Outdoors 37-53
7. Fun on the Farm 54-61
8. Creatures Great & Small 62-64
9. Hodgepodge Fun 65-70
10. Feeling Festive 71-76

Table of Contents

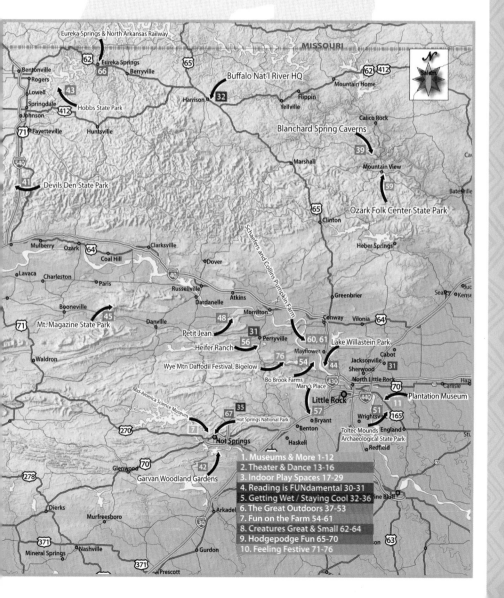

1. Museums & More 1-12
2. Theater & Dance 13-16
3. Indoor Play Spaces 17-29
4. Reading is FUNdamental 30-31
5. Getting Wet / Staying Cool 32-36
6. The Great Outdoors 37-53
7. Fun on the Farm 54-61
8. Creatures Great & Small 62-64
9. Hodgepodge Fun 65-70
10. Feeling Festive 71-76

Introduction

When I was four years old, my family moved to Little Rock. As the oldest of four siblings, I got very used to my parents driving us around the city and visiting locations around the state. I remember anxiously waiting in the elevator at Blanchard Springs Caverns as we went down into the earth. I remember that my family made sure we were never out of town on the weekend of the Greek Food Festival. I remember my dad taking me to the Mid-America Museum in Hot Springs every year after our camping trips.

I had the pleasure of growing up here. And what a pleasure it is to share my wonderful city with you! I hope that you'll use this book as a guide to exploring fun places and making lasting memories with your family and friends. This book is appropriate for children up to age twelve. I have included enough information for each location so that you can make an informed decision about whether it's right for your crew.

Take your time to soak in and benefit from each of these locations. I know we sure did! Discovering new places and uncovering new experiences are priceless to you and your child. Talk with them about what you've learned at each place, capture your memories in photos, and enjoy this fun city!

A few things to note:

• "Like" these locations on Facebook. It's a great way to keep up with events, promotions, and discounts.

• Call ahead—prices and hours are subject to change.

• Most of these playdate locations have birthday packages. Check out the websites or call to get more information.

• Before you visit any of these locations, check out the website to see if there are any passes or coupons available.

• If you find a place that you love, purchase a family membership. You'll likely end up spending more on a few visits than on a yearly membership. Most memberships offer benefits with free attendance at events.

• New sites? Corrections? Suggestions for the next edition? playdatelittlerock@gmail.com

Some details may change. Call ahead.
Use this book for ideas to expand your family fun!

How to Use this Guide

Each chapter is made up of a variety of places that are similar to one another. As you discover your child's interests, it will be easy to find several destinations in the area for exploration and discovery. Each description is similarly organized throughout the book.

Easy Reference to Site Number and City.

Color-Coordinated Chapters.

Address, Phone, Website.

Critical Site Information:
Hours, Admission, Membership, Parking, Food, Discounts.

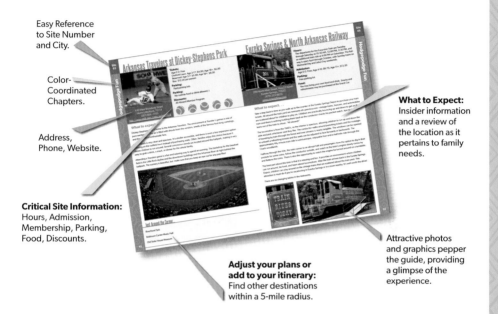

What to Expect:
Insider information and a review of the location as it pertains to family needs.

Adjust your plans or add to your itinerary:
Find other destinations within a 5-mile radius.

Attractive photos and graphics pepper the guide, providing a glimpse of the experience.

The Basics – Each destination's address, phone number, and website are listed for easy reference. Following that are hours, admission, membership information, parking, food policy, and information on obtaining discounts for places that charge admission. Remember, hours and prices may change, so call in advance. The referenced memberships and season passes are family memberships, usually for two adults and a certain number of children. Many locations offer free admission to children under a specific age. In those instances, you could purchase an individual or couple admission for a lower rate. Please note that this information is subject to change and we encourage you to check the location's website before departing.

What to Expect – A detailed description will help you decide whether a certain destination is right for your family. Information that is pertinent to parents of young children is included, such as whether restrooms include diaper-changing tables.

Annual Events – Many locations have special celebrations each year that are particularly child-friendly. Some events may celebrate a holiday like Halloween, while others may celebrate something about the facility like its anniversary.

Just Around the Corner – If you have a particularly energetic child, you may want to visit more than one destination in the same day. Maybe you just want to check out another destination on your way home from a favorite spot. Or perhaps you're considering a "staycation" this year and want a variety of activities in a specific part of town. This section will help you fulfill each of these goals. Sites are considered just around the corner if they're within approximately five miles of a given site.

Keep Your Bags Packed

If you intend to visit a wide variety of places, you might consider keeping a tote box in your trunk with essential items. Adjust the box when the weather changes and you'll always be prepared. (Note: If you use plastic water bottles, do not store them in the tote box, particularly in the summer. Studies have shown that the plastic can leach into the water when heated.)

Warm Weather Tote Box:

- ☐ Regular sunscreen
- ☐ Waterproof sunscreen
- ☐ Extra diapers and swim diapers
- ☐ Sun hats, swimsuits, towels, and a change of clothes for you and your child
- ☐ Beach toys like pails, shovels, rakes, sand shapers, and trucks
- ☐ Floaties, goggles, and other swimming accessories
- ☐ Baby powder (for sandbox play)
- ☐ Books, sidewalk chalk, and bubbles
- ☐ A washable tote bag for wet or sandy clothes
- ☐ Bandages and antibiotic cream (Neo to Go sprays on and won't spill in the tote)
- ☐ Insect repellent and anti-itch cream (try Benadryl on the Go for anti-itch)
- ☐ Individually-packaged, non-perishable snacks

Cold Weather Tote Box:

- ☐ Lip balm and lotion
- ☐ Sunscreen
- ☐ Extra diapers
- ☐ Extra sweatshirts, coats, hats, and gloves or mittens
- ☐ Short-sleeve shirts for you and your child, for those oddly warm days
- ☐ Snow boots
- ☐ Hand warmers
- ☐ Books, coloring books, and crayons
- ☐ A washable tote bag for wet or dirty clothes
- ☐ Bandages and antibiotic cream
- ☐ Individually-packaged non-perishable snacks

One of my favorite things to do with my children is to take them to museums. The museums in this chapter cover a wide range of ages and interests. Most have so many exhibits and galleries that they never seem to get old.

Courtesy of Arkansas Arts Center

Museums & More

Arkansas Arts Center

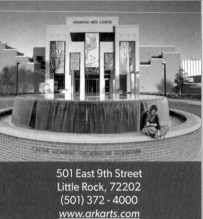

501 East 9th Street
Little Rock, 72202
(501) 372 - 4000
www.arkarts.com

Hours:
10:00 AM - 5:00 PM, Tuesday - Saturday
11:00 AM - 5:00 PM, Sunday.

Admission:
FREE!

Membership:
$75 for a family membership, which includes full
benefits - listed online for two adults and their children
or grandchildren, 17 and under.

Parking:
Free parking lot.

Food:
No outside food or drink allowed. Best Impressions
restaurant is open for lunch Tuesday - Sunday, 11:00
AM - 2:00 PM.

What to expect...

Founded in 1960, the Arkansas Arts
Center offers world-class art galleries,
lectures, films, art classes, theatre
productions, and family programs.
The exquisite interior of the museum
is spacious, with a unique design
that creates an unfettered feel—from
the glass windows around Best
Impressions restaurant to the colossal
skylights throughout the museum.

Many people would not consider
taking their children to an art
museum, but exposing your children
to art at a young age can help foster
appreciation. The museum offers

art classes for children and has exhibits that feature young artists. While this isn't somewhere I would
recommend bringing your rambunctious three-year-old, it is a great place to teach your elementary-aged
children about art. (And with the quiet atmosphere, it is the perfect haven for Mommy to strap the little
one in the stroller and spend some "alone" time admiring beautiful sculptures, watercolors, and other
unique pieces of art.)

Best Impressions restaurant is a great place to grab lunch. You can view the full menu online. Be sure to check
out the gift shop, which has an entire section devoted to puzzles, games, activity kits, finger puppets, and
other items that are perfect for children. A beautiful array of local glass work, pottery, and jewelry make this
museum gift shop one to spend some extra time in.

The women's restrooms have changing tables and are located on both floors of the museum.

Just Around the Corner...

Arkansas Repertory Theatre

Children's Theatre

Historic Arkansas Museum

Arkansas Inland Maritime Museum

120 Riverfront Park Drive
North Little Rock, 72114
(501) 371 - 8320
www.aimmmuseum.org

Hours:
10:00 AM - 6:00 PM, Friday - Saturday
1:00 PM - 6:00 PM, Sunday

Museum hours vary seasonally.

Admission:
Age 0-11: $4.00; Age 12-61: $6.00; Age 62+: $4.00;
Military: $4.00; Museum only (no submarine tour):
$2.00

Parking:
Free parking lot.

Food:
No outside food or drink allowed.

What to expect...

At the Arkansas Inland Maritime Museum, you can tour the USS Razorback, a veteran submarine from World War II, the Vietnam War, and the Cold War. This is a fascinating museum and the tour of the submarine is one of the most unique things you can do in Little Rock, but the museum recommends not bringing children under the age of five. Ladders, narrow passageways, and slippery surfaces can prove hazardous for a little one!

The museum houses a theater and a research library. Several outdoor exhibits, including the USS Snook Memorial, are worth exploring. The Beacon of Hope and Peace statue sits outside of the museum.

The museum store has plenty of memorabilia commemorating the USS Razorback. There are no changing tables in the restrooms.

Just Around the Corner...

Historic Arkansas Museum

Peabody Park

Riverfront Park

Arkansas State Capitol

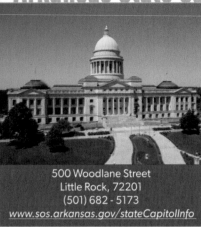

500 Woodlane Street
Little Rock, 72201
(501) 682 - 5173
www.sos.arkansas.gov/stateCapitolInfo

Hours:
8:00 AM - 5:00 PM, Monday - Friday
10:00 AM - 5:00 PM, Weekends

Admission:
FREE!

Parking:
Metered street parking and free parking available around the Capitol lawn.

Food:
You may bring your own food and drink, as long as you eat at the cafeteria located on the first floor or the snack area on the third floor.

What to expect...

With 247,000 square feet, 213 feet of open space between the ground floor and the 24-karat gold-leaf cupola, and multiple monuments and memorials, the grandeur of the Arkansas State Capitol will keep you and your children in awe. The interior of the building is made of marble and the exterior is made of limestone quarried in Batesville. The sweeping, manicured lawns and beautiful trees provide an idyllic foreground to the building.

One of my favorite times to visit the State Capitol is during the month of December, when the building is twinkling with Christmas lights and decorated inside and outside with elegant holiday décor. The capitol lighting ceremony takes place the first Saturday in December. You can call or check the website to find the holiday choir schedule; listening to the voices carol and echo off the marble is surreal. Take the time to walk up to the enormous, bronze doors and admire the brightly-illuminated building located at the very end of Capitol Avenue. The front entrance doors were purchased from Tiffany's in New York City for $10,000.00.

A great way to enjoy time with your children at the capitol is to pack a picnic lunch and observe the bustle of downtown from the capitol grounds. You can also contact the Secretary of State's office for a free, guided tour. These stroller-friendly tours are offered on weekdays from 9:00 AM - 4:00 PM. Call (501) 682 - 5080 to schedule. A gift shop, located on the first floor, offers capitol memorabilia as well as Arkansas-made crafts. It is open on weekdays from 9:00 AM - 4:00 PM. Restrooms are located in several areas of the building, with changing tables in both the men's and women's.

Just Around the Corner...

Mosaic Templars Cultural Center

Old State House Museum

Robinson Center Musical Hall

Historic Arkansas Museum

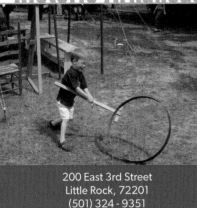

Hours:
9:00 AM - 5:00 PM, Monday - Saturday
1:00 PM - 5:00 PM, Sunday
Admission:
FREE!
Membership:
$50 for a family membership.
Tours:
Age 0-17: $1.00; Age 18-64: $2.50; Age 65+: $1.50
Parking:
Free parking lot.
Food:
No outside food or drink allowed.
Discounts:
Historic Homes Tours are free the first Sunday of each month.

200 East 3rd Street
Little Rock, 72201
(501) 324 - 9351
www.historicarkansas.org

What to expect...

Located in the heart of downtown Little Rock, the Historic Arkansas Museum offers adventurous and educational opportunities for children of all ages. The exhibits, art galleries, historic homes, and a fun room (devoted entirely to letting children play and explore) make this museum a great place to visit.

The Historic Homes Tours, which typically last one hour, depart hourly with the last tour departing at 4:00 PM. Tours between 10:00 AM and 3:00 PM include presentations by historical characters portrayed by actors. One of the homes featured on the tour is the oldest home in Arkansas! The tour is stroller-friendly, except for one house that is two stories high.

Two of the permanent exhibits are "History of the Bowie Knife," and "We Walk in Two Worlds." The "Bowie Knife" exhibit has touch screens that allow visitors to explore the history of knife making. "We Walk in Two Worlds" portrays Arkansas' first people: the Caddo, Osage, and Quapaw tribes. This exhibit is interactive, making it a great place to bring your children.

The Sturgis Children's Gallery alone makes this destination one to visit. Although not very large, it is rarely crowded. A photo booth for old-timey photos, a spyglass telescope, the Arkansas twister game, the Arkansas match game, a puppet theater, and a dirt detective table all make this room perfect for a playdate.

The museum is stroller-friendly, with elevators between the first and second floors. Make sure that you check out the museum store, which is stocked with Arkansas-made jewelry and pottery, as well as educational toys, music, quilts, and more. Restrooms are located throughout the museum, with changing tables in the women's restrooms.

Annual Events

Territorial Fair is the Saturday in May before Mother's Day.

Nog-off and **Christmas Frolic & Open House** are both in early December.

Just Around the Corner...

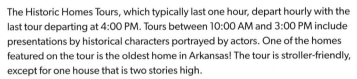

Museum of Discovery

River Rail

River Market District

Little Rock Central High School National Historic Site

Hours:
9:00 AM - 4:30 PM, daily
Tours are at 9:00 AM and 1:15 PM on weekdays.

Admission:
FREE!

Parking:
Free parking lot.

Food:
No outside food or drink allowed.

2120 Daisy L. Gatson Bates Drive
Little Rock, 72202
(501) 374 - 1957
www.nps.gov/chsc/index.htm

What to expect...

For parents with elementary-aged children or older, I highly recommend the Little Rock Central High School National Historic Site. The site is interactive, and provides an opportunity to not only explore an important part of Little Rock's history, but also to discuss issues like equality and racism with your children.

On weekdays, there are tours at 9:00 AM and 1:15 PM that last one hour and take you through Little Rock Central High School. These tours are child-friendly and stroller-friendly. The school is beautiful and simply magnificent in its grandeur. I highly recommend scheduling a tour.

The exhibit is not large but is packed with information and interactive touch screens offering unique testimonies and oral histories. Some of these accounts include bomb drills, teacher interactions, student interactions, harassment of students and parents, and graduation day. The exhibit is divided into three main sections: the history of race relations, the incident at Little Rock Central High School, and the positive impact for worldwide equality. While the exhibit deals with weighty issues, none are inappropriate. At the back of the exhibit, pictures depict the events that took place in the streets with the National Guard and the nine students. It is sobering to look out at the exact spot in front of the school, and imagine the events and emotions that day.

The exhibit is stroller-friendly. The touch screens, telephones, and displays are all interesting and interactive. The friendly staff members are more than happy to answer your questions. A small gift shop, located in the lobby, offers books and memorabilia related to Little Rock Central High School. There is a changing table in the women's restroom.

Just Around the Corner...

Arkansas Arts Center

Little Rock Zoo

War Memorial Park

MacArthur Museum of Arkansas Military History

Hours:
9:00 AM - 4:00 PM, Monday - Saturday
1:00 PM - 4:00 PM, Sunday

Admission:
FREE!

Parking:
Free parking lot.

Food:
No outside food or drink allowed.

503 East Ninth Street
Little Rock, 72202
(501) 376 - 4602
www.arkmilitaryheritage.com

What to expect...

Located in the historic Arsenal Building in MacArthur Park—one of Little Rock's oldest surviving structures and the birthplace of General Douglas MacArthur—the MacArthur Museum of Arkansas Military History is an exciting place to learn about Arkansas' military history.

Your children will learn how Arkansas has been involved in expeditions and wars. With exhibits ranging from the life of General MacArthur to ones highlighting weapons or wars, this museum is rich with fascinating information. The MacArthur Museum of Arkansas Military History is a great place to take a child who has expressed an interest in history.

There are no changing tables in the restrooms.

Just Around the Corner...

Arkansas Arts Center

Heifer Village

Historic Arkansas Museum

Mid-America Science Museum

500 Mid America Boulevard
Hot Springs, 71913
(501) 767 - 3461
www.midamericamuseum.org

Hours:
Memorial Day - Labor Day: 9:00 AM - 6:00 PM, daily
Labor Day - Memorial Day (fall/winter hours):
10:00 AM - 5:00 PM, Tuesday - Sunday

Admission:
Age 0-2: Free; Age 3-12: $7.00; Age 13-64: $9.00; Age
65+: $7.00, Military: $7.00

Membership:
$65.00 for a family membership includes two adults,
two children, and one guest.

Parking:
Free parking lot.

Food:
No outside food or drink allowed.

What to expect...

The Mid-America Science Museum was one of my favorite places when I was a child and is my favorite place in Hot Springs to take my children now! With hands-on exhibits, this museum ignites imaginations and fuels the thirst for learning.

Here are some of the incredible exhibits that your children will enjoy:

Light, located on the upper level, includes several exhibits. Make sure to check out the shadow trapper, where you can use light to literally trap your shadow!

The Underground Arkansas Cave, located on the middle level, is a gigantic indoor cave full of tunnels and slides. Try to hang on to the swinging bridge, maneuver your way up a rope ladder, and feel like a real caving adventurer!

Tesla Theater, located on the lower level, houses the world's most powerful conical Tesla Coil. This incredible show demonstrates the power of electricity! This show is very loud, so it might frighten little ones.

Structures, located on the lower level, is a great place to learn how structures can withstand the force of gravity. Move a building wall, and build supporting structures for bridges, buildings, and arches!

Tinkering Studio, located on the lower level, is a space designed to let your children's creativity run wild. The studio offers a vast array of hands-on activities, crafts, and projects. Your little ones are sure to enjoy this!

Outside of the museum, a paved nature trail and a Cretaceous Park lets you become a paleontologist. Children can search for dinosaur footprints and uncover a raptor skeleton!

The museum store is fantastic—full of science kits, educational toys, books, and just about anything you can imagine that supports science and young minds. The store carries well-known, educational product lines, such as: Green Science Kits, Kinetics, Frigits, Earthopoly, and Thames & Kosmos Science Kits. There are changing tables in the women's restrooms, located on both floors of the museum.

Museums & More

Mosaic Templars Cultural Center

Hours:
9:00 AM - 5:00 PM, Tuesday - Saturday

Admission:
FREE!

Parking:
Free parking lot.

Food:
No outside food or drink allowed.

501 West Ninth Street
Little Rock, 72201
(501) 683 - 3593
www.mosaictemplarscenter.com

What to expect...

"The mission of the Mosaic Templars Cultural Center is to collect, preserve, interpret and celebrate Arkansas' African-American history, culture and community from 1870 to the present, and to inform and educate the public about black achievement—especially in business, politics, and the arts."

On October 15, 1913, Booker T. Washington dedicated this building in front of 2,000 people. While the original building was destroyed by a fire in 2005, the Department of Arkansas Heritage built a new structure in 2006 on the original site. This quiet museum isn't the place to bring your four-year-old. However, the Mosaic Templars Cultural Center is a beautiful building, housing both the center and the Arkansas Black Hall of Fame. This would be a great place to bring your child in conjunction with the Little Rock Central High School National Historic Site.

The permanent exhibits include: Brotherhood and the Bottom Line: The Mosaic Templars of America; Entrepreneurial Spirit; A City Within a City, Little Rock's West Ninth Street Business District; A Building for the Community, The History of the Mosaic Templars of America Building, African Americans in Arkansas 1870-1970, and the Arkansas Black Hall of Fame.

You can call in advance for a free, guided tour. Make sure to check out the museum store, which has a great collection of children's books. The museum hosts family fun days and activities for children, so check the website for upcoming events. The women's restroom has a changing table.

Just Around the Corner...

Arkansas Arts Center

Arkansas State Capitol

Old State House Museum

Museum of Discovery

500 President Clinton Avenue, Suite 150
Little Rock, 72201
(501) 396 - 7050
www.museumofdiscovery.org

Hours:
9:00 AM - 5:00 PM, Tuesday - Saturday
1:00 PM - 5:00 PM, Sunday

Admission:
Age 0-11 months: Free; Age 1-12, teachers, active/re-
tired military, and seniors (60+): $8; Adults: $10

Membership:
$85 for a family membership, which includes two adults
and three children.

Parking:
Parking in the River Market District.

Food:
No outside food or drink allowed.

What to expect...

The Museum of Discovery is Little Rock's oldest museum, although its complete remodel in 2011 might disguise this fact. The museum is fundamentally interactive and is the perfect place to bring your children, no matter their age. You will all have a great time and learn a thing or two.

Check out these features of the museum:

Amazing You! is an exhibit devoted to the human body. You can examine teeth under a microscope, figure out how healthy your dinner is or how much blood you have in your body, and hear a drum set play your heartbeat.

Discovery Hall is devoted to hands-on exhibits that center on how we can understand math and physics in our environments. The exhibits teach about such things as force and energy.

Earth Journeys is a great place to learn about tornados, earthquakes, earth's composition, and some of Arkansas' unique geographic features. In Tornado Alley Theater, you can watch the true power of tornadoes. The movie is very loud, so you might not want to take your little ones inside the theater.

Room to Grow is a room for children ages six and under. In other words: you don't have to worry about "big kids" running around your little ones! From an enormous pirate ship and tree house to a book corner, a wall of magnets, and a theater with a neon-glowing piano, your little ones will be entertained for hours!

Tinkering Studio is open all day on Saturday and Sunday and from 2:00 PM - 4:30 PM on Tuesday through Friday. Here, museum visitors get to experiment with various building techniques in a collaborative environment.

Check out the museum's website for information on upcoming exhibits, science theater shows, and much more!

Just Around the Corner...

River Rail

William J. Clinton Presidential Library and Museum

Witt Stephens Jr. Central Arkansas Nature Center

Old State House Museum

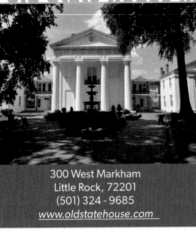

300 West Markham
Little Rock, 72201
(501) 324 - 9685
www.oldstatehouse.com

Hours:
9:00 AM - 5:00 PM, Monday - Saturday
1:00 PM - 5:00 PM, Sunday

Admission:
FREE!

Parking:
Metered parking is available around the museum. One hour of free parking is available at the garage beneath the Double Tree Hotel; bring your parking ticket to the museum for validation.

Food:
No outside food or drink allowed.

What to expect...

"The capitol should be near, and . . . in view of the river. A State House, built with taste and elegance . . . would command the admiration and respect of the passing stranger, and have a moral and political influence on the whole community." -Territorial Governor John Pope, 1842.

Constructed in 1888, the Old State House Museum is the oldest standing state capitol building west of the Mississippi River. The museum was the location for President Bill Clinton's election night celebrations in 1992 and 1996. The Old State House Museum is a designated National Historic Landmark.

While there are temporary exhibits at the museum, the permanent exhibits include: Arkansas' First Families, 1836 House of Representatives Chamber, Pillars of Power, Whistle Stop Station (a hands-on children's area), and As Long As Life Shall Last: The Legacy of Arkansas Women. You can call ahead to schedule a guided tour. If you want to explore on your own, the museum offers self-guided cell phone tours. Guided tours are offered every hour on the hour, with the last tour starting at 4:00 PM.

The museum offers special programs for children. Consult the website to find out about upcoming events. Make sure to check out the museum store. With beautiful jewelry and a variety of books and gifts, it's definitely worth your time. The women's restroom has a changing table.

Annual Events

Big BOO!-seum Bash: Don a costume and enjoy games, crafts, and tasty treats!

Holiday Open House: Get in the holiday spirit by making ornaments and paper snowflakes while enjoying caroling and cookies!

Just Around the Corner...

Arkansas State Capitol

Peabody Park

Robinson Center Music Hall

Plantation Agriculture Museum

Hours:
8:00 AM - 5:00 PM, Tuesday - Saturday
1:00 PM - 5:00, Sunday

Admission:
FREE!

Parking:
Free parking lot.

Food:
No outside food or drink allowed.

4815 Ark.161 South
Scott, 72142
(501) 961 - 1409
www.arkansasstateparks.com

What to expect...

The Plantation Agriculture Museum in Scott is dedicated to Arkansas' cotton agriculture heritage and is definitely worth the thirty-minute drive from Little Rock. In June 1989, after years of neglect, the museum reopened with a newly-stated mission to "collect, preserve, record, and interpret the history of cotton agriculture, with an emphasis on plantations."

The museum has more than 10,000 artifacts, and houses exhibits that range from explanations of how cotton was grown to exploring the lives of slaves, sharecroppers, and plantation owners. Outside the museum, at the 1912 Dortch Gin Building and the Seed Warehouse, you can tour a cotton gin and cotton press. Tractor exhibits and a patch of cotton are spread around the museum.

The museum and grounds are stroller-friendly. There is a changing table in the women's restroom.

William J. Clinton Presidential Library and Museum

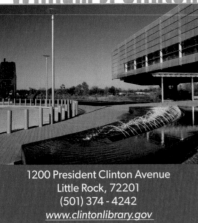

1200 President Clinton Avenue
Little Rock, 72201
(501) 374 - 4242
www.clintonlibrary.gov

Hours:
9:00 AM - 5:00 PM, Monday - Saturday
1:00 PM - 5:00 PM, Sunday

Admission:
Age 0-5: Free; Age 6-17: $3.00; Age 18-61: $7.00; Age 62+: $5.00

Discounts:
College students with valid ID: $5.00; Retired military: $5.00; Active duty military: Free

Parking:
Free parking lot.

Food:
No outside food or drink allowed.

What to expect...

The William J. Clinton Presidential Library and Museum is a wonderful place to bring children to see world-class exhibits and to partake in tours, activities, camps, and programs. The educational programs are designed to expand your children's talents, interests, and ideas. Check the website for upcoming programs.

Guided tours require reservations two weeks in advance, however, you can take a self-guided tour through the museum and library. The library holds over 100,000 items that were given to President Clinton during his two terms as president. From exploring these fascinating items to seeing the oval office as it looked during Clinton's presidency, this museum is definitely one worth visiting!

The museum grounds are an ideal place to let the kids run around or to enjoy a picnic. They also serve as the location for the library's annual Easter egg hunt. The museum always hosts a variety of events and exhibits. The museum's website or Facebook page allows you to stay up-to-date on discounted days and exciting events. The women's restroom has a changing table.

Just Around the Corner...

Heifer Village

River Rail

Witt Stephens Jr. Central Arkansas Nature Center

Lights, camera, action! If your child is old enough to sit still through a play, you should absolutely take her to one! Plays can ignite imagination and curiosity— literally bringing stories to life. Make sure to "like" each of these places on Facebook so that you have an easy way of keeping up with upcoming productions. Experience the magic of live theater with your child!

Courtesy of Childrens's Theatre

Arkansas Repertory Theatre

501 East 9th Street
Little Rock, 72202
(501) 372 - 4000
www.therep.org

Season:
Season runs from September through June, with seven to eight main stage productions.

Shows:
Performances are typically Wednesday through Sunday, with matinees at 2:00 PM on Sundays and evening performances at 7:00 PM or 8:00 PM.

Tickets:
Ticket prices vary from $20.00 to $60.00 depending on show, time, and date.

Parking:
Metered street parking and pay-in-advance parking lots.

Food:
No outside food or drink allowed. Snacks and beverages are sold before and after the performance as well as during intermission.

Discounts:
"Pay What You Can Night" is typically the first night that a play opens. The tickets are first-come, first-served, and are limited to two per person. Check the theatre's website for a complete listing of the year's "Pay What You Can Night" dates.

What to expect...

Nestled in a building on the corner of one of downtown's busiest streets is a place where magic happens, worlds blossom, and imaginations are ignited. "The Rep," as locals call the Arkansas Repertory Theatre, is one of my favorite places to catch a play in Little Rock. The first plays began in 1976, and now The Rep is Arkansas' largest non-profit professional theatre, playing host to nearly 70,000 individuals annually.

Make sure to check the schedule online to see when plays are showing. Every year a few of the plays cater to younger audiences; consequently, The Rep is a popular place for school groups to visit. New performances are shown every month, with a Christmas play showing the entire month of December. Since I was a little girl, we have gone as a family every December to watch plays like *A Christmas Carol* and *It's A Wonderful Life*.

The Rep displays local artists' work. During intermission or before the show, you can browse and admire the artwork while you're enjoying a drink or a cookie. The greatest aspects of the Rep are twofold. First, you're guaranteed to see a great play. Second, if you live in Little Rock, you should take your children to experience the "local" aspect of the theatre. The Rep is such a staple of Little Rock that it is sure to not be your last time to go.

Just Around the Corner...

Arkansas Arts Center

Children's Theatre

Mosaic Templars Cultural Center

Murry's Dinner Playhouse

6323 Colonel Glenn Road
Little Rock, 72204
(501) 562 - 3131
www.murrysdinnerplayhouse.com

Hours:
Tuesday - Saturday:
Dinner at 6:00 PM - 7:35 PM and curtain at 7:45 PM.

Sunday and Wednesday matinees: Lunch at 11:00 AM - 12:40 PM and curtain at 12:45 PM.

Wednesday matinees: Occur only on the first, second, and third Wednesdays of each new production.

Sunday: Dinner at 5:30 PM - 6:40 PM and curtain at 6:45 PM.

Admission:
Age 0-15: $23.00 ; Show only kids: $15.00;
Show only adults: $25.00; Matinees and preview nights: $29.00; Sunday - Thursday: $31.00; Friday and Saturday: $33.00.

Parking:
Free parking lot.

Food:
No outside food or drink allowed.

What to expect...

Be ready for a delicious meal and a wonderful play whenever you visit Murry's Dinner Playhouse. The atmosphere is very intimate, making this a great place for a special time with your family. Due to the size of the playhouse and proximity to the stage, this is not the place to bring a little one who can't sit still and enjoy the show.

Although most of the plays at Murry's are geared toward an adult audience, usually at least one play each season is appropriate for children. The theater, which opened its doors in 1967, plays host to spectacular shows and is a member of the National Dinner Theatre Association. The season runs from late April through December.

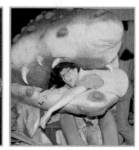

Just Around the Corner...

Arkansas Skatium

Playtime Pizza

Play Tubes at Rock Creek

Children's Theatre

Season:
Season runs from mid-September through mid-May, with six main stage productions. Each production generally runs for two weeks.

Shows:
Friday: 7:00 PM; Saturday: 3:00 PM; Sunday: 2:00 PM

Tickets:
Age 0-2: Free; Age 3+: $12.00

Parking:
Free parking lot.

Food:
No outside food or drink allowed.

501 East 9th Street
Little Rock, 72202
(501) 372 - 4000
www.arkarts.com/childrens_theatre

What to expect…

Children's Theatre, a part of the Arkansas Arts Center, is the only professional company in Arkansas that produces child-directed works for the stage. It has been drawing audiences of parents and children since 1979. Contemporary stories and classics alike come to life on the stage. With elaborate costumes and sets, as well as fantastic characters, magical productions such as James and the Giant Peach and The Princess and the Pea , the theatre is sure to spark your child's imagination and curiosity. It is no wonder the Children's Theatre is popular with school groups.

The plays usually last one hour and fifteen minutes with no intermission. All seating is general admission and begins a half hour before the play, so make sure to get there early to get good seats! Restrooms with changing tables are located inside the Arkansas Arts Center.

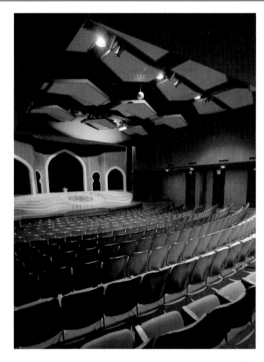

Just Around the Corner...

Arkansas Arts Center

Arkansas Repertory Theatre

River Rail

Robinson Center Music Hall

Tickets:
Ticket prices vary.

Parking:
Paid parking available in the parking garage located by the Double Tree Hotel.

Food:
No outside food or drink allowed.

426 West Markham
Little Rock, 72201
(501) 376 - 4781
TicketMaster handles scheduling.

What to expect...

With the capacity to seat 2,609 individuals, Robinson Center Music Hall is a grand proscenium arch hall with a sweeping balcony and enormous stage. Not all performances are for children, but the ones that are age-appropriate are worth attending. The hall regularly plays host to traveling Broadway shows, the Arkansas Symphony Orchestra, and various performing artists. Each December, the Arkansas Symphony Orchestra puts on a spectacular holiday show!

Drinks and snacks are usually sold at intermission. The restrooms do not have changing tables.

Just Around the Corner...

Arkansas State Capitol

Old State House Museum

River Rail

Indoor Play Spaces

Let's be honest—we live in a climate of extreme weather conditions here in the Natural State. Often, it's either "a million degrees outside" or you're "freezing to death." These indoor places offer fun ways for your little ones to get all their energy out with no need to go stir-crazy at home!

Courtesy of Firefly

All Aboard Restaurant and Grill

Hours:
10:30 AM - 8:00 PM, daily for lunch and dinner.

Parking:
Free parking lot.

Discounts:
All Aboard Member Program

6813 Cantrell Road
Little Rock, 72207
(501) 975 - 7401
www.all-aboardrestaurant.com

What to expect...

All Aboard Restaurant and Grill is a family-friendly restaurant, with a fun atmosphere and courteous wait staff. The popularity of the restaurant stems from the intricate train and rail system that delivers delicious food to your table!

All Aboard is perfect for a meal before or after a playdate. From hamburgers and home-cut fries to a strawberry salad and veggie wrap, the menu features choices that will make adults and children happy. Organic and locally-grown ingredients are frequently used. For discounts on meals, join the All Aboard Member Program, which is available through their website.

The booths do not seat more than four or five people comfortably, so for bigger groups, be prepared to sit at different tables.

Just Around the Corner...

Big Dam Bridge

Painted Pig Studio

Murray Park

Altitude Trampoline Park

15707 Chenal Pkw,
Little Rock, AR 72211
(479) 763-JUMP
www.altitudetrampolineparklr.com

Hours:
10:00 AM - 9:00 PM, Monday - Thursday
10:00 AM - 11:00 PM, Friday
9:00 AM - 11:00 PM, Saturday
12:00 PM - 8:00 PM, Sunday

Admission:
Single jumper: 1hr ($12.75); 2hr ($21.00); 3hr ($27.00).

Family Fun Jump : 2 adults, 2 children $29.95 , 1hr jump pass.

Toddler Time (10:00 - 1:00 M-F) $6.95 or $8.95 with adult.

2 & under: always free.

Food:
No outside food or drink allowed.

What to expect...

One of Little Rock's newest locations to have fun, Altitude Trampoline Park is a perfect place for an exciting (and bouncy) playdate. While this would not be the best place to bring your one-year-old, it's perfect for toddlers on up. They have over two hundred interconnected trampolines and the state's largest foam pit!

Make sure that your children are wearing comfortable clothes that they can bounce around in. Shoes are not allowed on the trampoline, so they'll be jumping in either socks or bare feet. Also, no jewelry allowed! Parents, you will have to sign a waiver for your children to jump on the trampolines.

You don't need to worry about your three-year-old being bounced sky-high by a teenager, as Altitude Trampoline Park has a Kids Zone—where you must be under 80 pounds to jump. And with safety netting, padding (no gaps or exposed springs on the trampolines), and soft trampoline walls, this is a great place to let your children have a fun time and get all their energy out!

Just Around the Corner...

Altitude Trampoline Park

Barnes & Noble

Playtime Pizza

Play Tubes at Rock Creek

Arkansas Skatium Ice Rink

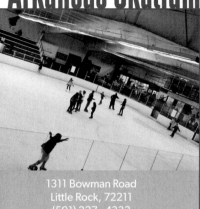

1311 Bowman Road
Little Rock, 72211
(501) 227 - 4333
www.arkansasskatium.com

Hours:
1:00 PM - 3:30 PM, Tuesday
1:00 PM - 3:30 PM and 7:30 PM - 10:00 PM, Friday
2:00 PM - 4:00 PM and 7:00 PM - 10:00 PM, Saturday
2:00 PM - 5:00 PM, Sunday

Admission:
Age 0-4: Free with one paid admission; $8.00 if you have your own skates; $11.00 if you need to rent skates; $12.00 for both ice and roller skating.

Parking:
Free parking lot.

Food:
No outside food or drink allowed. A concession stand offers food and cold drinks, as well as hot beverages such as cappuccino, hot chocolate, and coffee.

What to expect...

Whether you're going to ice skate as a family or cheer your children on from the side, you're sure to have a great time at the Arkansas Skatium Ice Rink. The ice rink is large with plenty of seating in case you choose not to brave the ice.

Be prepared for the cold by bundling up! A hat, gloves, and a thick jacket are good ways to prevent teeth from chattering and prompting an early departure because someone is freezing. Thankfully, you can purchase a hot drink to warm you up if you get too cold. Every couple of hours, the ice has to be resurfaced and it's the perfect time to go grab a snack.

In a state like Arkansas, there aren't any ponds or lakes which freeze over in the winter, so the ice rink is a fun way to either cool off in the summer or to enjoy a wintry activity in the cold months. We always go during the month of December when the ice rink has special holiday hours. It's just the thing to put us in the holiday spirit!

The Arkansas Skatium offers ice skating classes and hockey classes for children. Check out their website for more information. Restrooms lack changing tables.

Just Around the Corner...

Altitude Trampoline Park

Arkansas Skatium Roller Rink

Barnes & Noble

Playtime Pizza

Play Tubes at Rock Creek

Arkansas Skatium Roller Rink

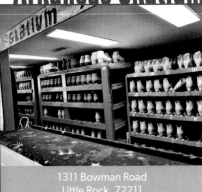

1311 Bowman Road
Little Rock, 72211
(501) 227 - 4333
www.arkansasskatium.com

Hours:
7:00 PM - 10:00 PM, Tuesday
7:30 PM - 10:00 PM, Friday
1:00 PM - 5:00 PM and 7:00 PM - 10:00 PM, Saturday
2:00 PM - 5:00 PM, Sunday

Admission:
Age 0-4: Free with one paid admission; $8.00 if you
have your own skates; $10.00 if you need to rent skates;
$12.00 for both ice and roller skating.

Parking:
Free parking lot.

Food:
No outside food or drink allowed.

Discounts:
On Tuesdays, admission is $4.50.

What to expect...

Growing up, I attended dozens of birthday parties at the Arkansas Skatium Roller Rink. With loud music, fun lights, and a huge rink, it was always a blast! The building has an aged feel, but the roller skating is still as entertaining and exciting as ever.

The Skatium offers "Moms and Tots" days on the third Friday of each month from September through May. From 10:00 AM - 12:00 PM, you can bring anything with wheels—strollers, wagons, scooters, whatever! The cost is only $4.00 per child. I recommend taking full advantage of this, especially since the Skatium is mostly open in the evenings.

Seating is available all around the skating rink, so it's easy to keep an eye on your children. A small concession stand offers snacks and drinks. Restrooms do not have changing tables.

Just Around the Corner...

Altitude Trampoline Park

Arkansas Skatium Ice Rink

Barnes & Noble

Playtime Pizza

Play Tubes at Rock Creek

Firefly Studio

Hours:
10:00 AM - 6:00 PM, Monday - Thursday
10:00 AM - 8:00 PM, Friday - Saturday
2:00 PM - 6:00 PM, Sunday

Admission:
Cost is based on the craft you choose.

Parking:
Free parking lot.

Food:
No outside food or drink allowed.

10700 North Rodney Parham Road, B5
Little Rock, 72212
(501) 225 - 1403
www.paintatfirefly.com

CRAFTS!

What to expect...

With over 300 craft options and 100 paint colors to choose from, you're sure to find something fun to paint at Firefly Studio. The relaxed atmosphere and convenient location just off Interstate-430 make this a great place to take the children for a memorable playdate. Firefly is very close to several kid-friendly restaurants, so you can grab lunch after you paint!

The friendly staff is more than willing to help you—from picking out paint colors to helping you get a hand or footprint out of your wriggling one-year-old. You need to leave the pottery for about a week (sometimes longer during holidays) to be fired. This is a great place to make Christmas ornaments, presents for grandparents, or to paint a mug for Father's Day. There are restrooms in the studio with a changing table.

Firefly Studio is an inviting place for little ones to explore their creativity in a colorful (and messy) way!

Just Around the Corner...

Professor Bowl

Two Rivers Park

The Wonder Place

Jump Zone

9250 Commerce Cove
North Little Rock, 72113
(501) 907 - 5867
www.jumpzoneparty.com

Hours:
10:00 AM - 5:00 PM and 6:00 PM - 9:00 PM, Friday
6:00 PM - 9:00 PM, Saturday
5:00 PM - 8:00 PM, Sunday

Admission:
Age 0-23 months: Free with one paid admission; Age 2+: $8.00; Parents: Free

Parking:
Free parking lot.

Food:
No outside food or drink allowed.

What to expect...

In 2010, Jump Zone was voted Runner Up as "Best Party Location" by *Savvy Kids* and it's easy to see why. With bouncy inflatable houses and inflatable slides everywhere, this is the perfect place for your children to expend lots of energy! Jump Zone offers snack, drink, and food options as well—anything from Icees and ice cream to pizza.

The inflatables include an enormous T-Rex, a dual spiral slide, a slide and challenge course, a carousel bouncy house, a basketball bouncy house, and a sinking ship. Participating children must wear socks. The women's restroom has a changing table.

Every Friday night from 6:00 - 9:00 is Family Fun Night, when admission for two children, a large pizza, and a two-liter drink costs $26.00. Family Fun Night is a great way to spend some time together doing something fun, and Mom doesn't have to worry about cooking dinner!

Just Around the Corner...

All Aboard Restaurant and Grill

Big Dam Bridge

Little Rock Zoo

Little Rock Climbing Center

12120 Colonel Glenn Road, #7000
Little Rock, 72210
(501) 227 - 9500
www.littlerockclimbingcenter.com

Hours:
12:00 PM - 10:00 PM, Monday, Wednesday, Friday
2:00 PM - 10:00 PM, Tuesday, Thursday
10:00 AM - 10:00 PM, Saturday
12:00 PM - 8:00 PM, Sunday

Admission:
Child Day Pass (age 5-12): $10.00; Adult Day Pass:
$12.00

Membership:
One month paid in full: Adults $50.00 and youth $45.00,
with $25.00 for gear rental.

Three months paid in full: Adults $140.00 and youth
$125.00, with $60.00 for gear rental.

Parking:
Free parking lot.

Food:
No outside food or drink allowed, except water.

Discounts:
Little Rock Climbing Center offers daily specials. Just
check the website to see all their deals! The military
discount is 10%.

What to expect...

Fighting gravity at the Little Rock Climbing Center
should provide loads of fun! This is a great way for
kids five and over to build strength, confidence, and
communication skills. The staff will show you exactly
how to climb safely. For climbers under the age of 18,
a parent or guardian must sign a waiver for emergency
information and liability release. Children under age 13
will need an adult to belay them, and anyone under the
age of 16 needs an adult to stay with them while they
climb.

If it's your first time climbing, check out the "First Time Climbers" section on their website. You'll have a
better idea of what to expect.

Little Rock Climbing Center offers birthday parties, summer camps, and climbing teams for children age
seven and older. They also offer a JV climbing team and a competitive climbing team. Summer climbing
camps fill up fast, so sign up early!

There are no changing tables in the restrooms. They do sell snacks and drinks, in case you forget to bring
some water. And trust me, you will work up a sweat!

Just Around the Corner...

Arkansas Skatium Ice Rink

Arkansas Skatium Roller Rink

Playtime Pizza

Play Tubes at Rock Creek

Millennium Bowl

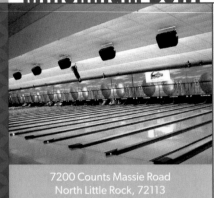

7200 Counts Massie Road
North Little Rock, 72113
(501) 791 - 9150
www.millenniumbowl.net

Hours:
9:00 AM - Close, Monday - Saturday
12:00 PM - Close, Sunday

Admission:
Monday - Friday before 5:00 PM: $3.40 per game per person or $18.00 per hour

Monday - Friday after 5:00 PM and Saturday - Sunday: $3.90 per game per person or $22.00 per hour

Parking:
Free parking lot.

Food:
No outside food or drink allowed.

What to expect...

Located in North Little Rock, Millennium Bowl is a newer bowling alley with 32 lanes. Bumpers are available so that children don't toss gutter balls. They also provide lighter balls to make bowling easier for little ones. A snack bar offers more than just snacks—you could easily eat lunch here with menu items from pizza and corndogs to chicken tenders and French fries. Since the bowling alley gets very popular in the evenings, you might want to go earlier in the day to avoid the adult crowd.

Millennium Bowl hosts birthday parties (check out the "Parties" section on their website for more information). They also offer a youth league for ages 3-21, at 10:00 AM on Saturdays in the fall. The women's restroom has a changing table. The tables, seating, and atmosphere are great!

Just Around the Corner...

Big Dam Bridge

Jump Zone

Lake Willastein Park

The Painted Pig

5622 R Street
Little Rock, 72207
(501) 280 – 0553
www.paintedpigstudio.com

Hours:
10:00 AM - 6:00 PM, Monday - Saturday
Last painters seated at 5:00 PM.

Admission:
Cost is based on the craft you choose.

Parking:
Free parking lot.

Food:
You may bring your own food and drink.

What to expect…

Let the creative juices flow at the Painted Pig—a place where you and your kids can get messy and have something cute to show for it! There are nearly endless options for items to paint and colors to choose. The Painted Pig has a wall dedicated to different paint colors and the friendly employees will be more than happy to let you know which colors go best together.

The atmosphere is very kid-friendly. With a wide array of options to fit any budget, your kids will be in artistic paradise. Paint covers the tables, so it's okay to make a mess! High chairs and booster seats accommodate younger children. I took my son to create a tile of his handprint, and employees (adept at working with children) were able to press my son's hand into the tile for me. Yay for not having to tackle your two-year-old!

The open layout provides ample room for a stroller, and the restroom features a changing table. If you go around lunchtime, head next door to Burge's—a famous Little Rock eatery and yet another place where it's okay to be loud and messy!

Just Around the Corner...

All Aboard Restaurant and Grill

Big Dam Bridge

Little Rock Zoo

Playtime Pizza

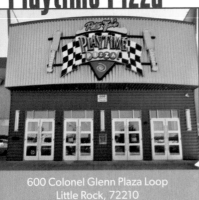

600 Colonel Glenn Plaza Loop
Little Rock, 72210
(501) 227 - 7529
www.playtimepizza.com

Hours:
4:00 PM - 9:00 PM, Monday - Wednesday
11:00 AM - 9:00 PM, Thursday
11:00 AM - 10:00 PM, Friday - Saturday
11:00 AM - 9:00 PM, Sunday

Admission:
Age 0-3: Free; Age 4-11: $6.99; Age 12+: $8.99

Parking:
Free parking lot.

Food:
No outside food or drink allowed.

What to expect...

With go-karts, laser tag, bumper cars, bowling, mini golf, an arcade, and a big buffet, there's no shortage of fun things to do at Playtime Pizza! The Pirates' Treasure Mini Golf is a perfect activity for the whole family to enjoy together. Children must be 48" tall to drive the bumper cars and 42" tall to ride. The Darklight Laser Tag has an minimum age requirement of eight, and the indoor go-kart racing has a height requirement of 54" to drive and 36" to ride. Playtime Pizza offers a large arcade with a variety of games and a great selection of prizes.

Additionally, a toddler room has padded mats and age-appropriate toys.

The buffet is full of choices: a pizza bar, a potato and soup bar, a pasta bar, a taco and nacho bar, a salad bar, and a dessert bar. So, you can have fun and eat yummy food! What could be better?

Just Around the Corner...

Arkansas Skatium Ice Rink

Arkansas Skatium Roller Rink

Murry's Dinner Playhouse

Play Tubes at Rock Creek

PLAYTIME
PRiZE GALLERY

Play Tubes at Rock Creek

Hours:
8:00 AM - 5:00 PM, Monday - Friday
Closed Friday 11:30 AM - 1:00 PM

The second Monday of every month, the tubes do not open until 1:00 PM.

Admission:
FREE!

Parking:
Free parking lot.

Food:
You may bring your own food and drink. Benches and chairs are available.

11500 West 36th Street
Little Rock, 72211
(501) 225-8684
www.churchatrockcreek.com

What to expect...

The Play Tubes at Rock Creek is a popular place for parents to take their children. The tubes are housed inside the Church at Rock Creek, but are open to the public on weekdays. Elevator access makes it easy to bring a stroller. Benches and seats are available for parents to relax on while children expend energy climbing through the two-story-high maze of tubes. Surrounded by windows, the attraction has an open, adventurous feel.

A play area for smaller children includes wall puzzles, a table with toys, and a squishy slide to crawl on. You can keep your children entertained here, regardless of age.

The tubes are a guaranteed place to have fun, but it is especially good when it's scorching or freezing outside. The best time to beat the crowds is first thing in the morning. The parking lot is big, so parking is rarely an issue. The women's restroom has a changing table.

Just Around the Corner...

Altitude Trampoline Park

Arkansas Skatium Roller Rink

Arkansas Skatium Ice Rink

Barnes & Noble

Playtime Pizza

Professor Bowl

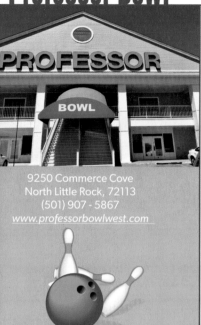

9250 Commerce Cove
North Little Rock, 72113
(501) 907 - 5867
www.professorbowlwest.com

Hours:
10:00 AM - 12:00 AM, Monday - Thursday
10:00 AM - 2:00 AM, Friday - Saturday
12:00 PM - 12:00 AM, Sunday

Admission:
Open bowling: $3.75 per game
Hourly open bowling rate: $21.00
Shoe rental: $2.25

Parking:
Free parking lot.

Food:
No outside food or drink allowed.

Discounts:
On Sundays, the price is $5.50 per person (includes 2 games and shoes).

The Kids Bowl Free program (www.kidsbowlfree.com) goes from the beginning of May through the end of October at specific days and times.

What to expect...

With 36 lanes, a full snack and food bar, and a game room, Professor Bowl is a fun place to take the whole family. The bowling alley becomes popular in the evenings, so the best time to take children is earlier in the day to avoid the adult crowd. Professor Bowl offers lighter balls and can put bumpers on the lanes.

The bowling alley offers birthday parties (see information on their website). I attended birthday parties here when I was little, if that gives you an idea of how long this place has been around! Changing tables are in the women's restroom.

Bowling is a fun way to relax and to spend time with friends or family. This is a playdate location that your little ones are sure to enjoy!

Just Around the Corner...

All Aboard Restaurant and Grill

Firefly Studio

The Wonder Place

The Wonder Place

Hours:
9:00 AM - 5:00 PM, Monday - Saturday

Admission:
$7 per person (second adult in the family is free)

Parking:
Free parking lot.

Food:
You may bring your own food and drink for the designated cafeteria area.

10301 North Rodney Parham
Little Rock, 72227
(501) 225 - 4050
www.thewonderplace.com

What to expect...

Designed for children age eight and under, The Wonder Place offers enough activities to keep your children playing and laughing for hours (and ready for an extra-long nap)! From an enormous water table, to a theater with every costume your child can imagine, to a market with shopping carts, food, and a register, plenty of excitement awaits!

The Wonder Place is spread throughout several rooms. A play area, located by the entrance and gift shop, is

designed for children age two and under. Snacks or lunch can be enjoyed at a perfect dining spot (furnished with high chairs) at the back of The Wonder Place.

An art room with crafts, a vet's office with stuffed animals and an x-ray machine, and a large play area designed to look like a tree house provide imaginative activities for your child. My oldest son's two favorite stations at the Wonder Place are the sand table and the water area. When we leave, he is messy. But is it worth it? Totally! And the best part is that when you pay, you can come and go for the rest of the day. So come in the morning, go home for a nap, and come back in the afternoon. You might want to pack a towel and extra wipes.

Just Around the Corner...

All Aboard Restaurant and Grill

The Painted Pig

Professor Bowl

4

Reading is FUNdamental

There is no better way to expand your child's mind, equip them for success, and engage them in other worlds, cultures, and environments than to give them a love of books and reading (says the girl who majored in English)! Check out all the events and activities taking place at the local libraries in the Central Arkansas Library System. There are fun things to do for any age!

Courtesy of Emily Benton Ryan

Reading is FUNdamental

Barnes & Noble

Hours:
9:00 AM - 10:00 PM, Monday - Thursday
9:00 AM - 11:00 PM, Friday - Saturday
9:00 AM - 9:00 PM, Sunday

Parking:
Free parking lot.

Food:
No outside food or drink allowed.

11500 Financial Centre Parkway
Little Rock, 72211
(501) 954 - 7646
www.barnesandnoble.com

What to expect...

The children's section in Barnes & Noble is second to none. With a small stage for playing, a train table, and thousands of books to browse, it's a great place to ignite your child's interest in reading and learning. Barnes & Noble has recently added a game section with a wide variety of toys and games. I peruse the bargain books for gifts—the selection is great!

Barnes & Noble has a story time specifically for children. Call to find out when these are offered. A Starbucks is located within the store, and the women's restroom at the back of the bookstore has a changing table.

Just Around the Corner...

Altitude Trampoline Park

Arkansas Skatium Ice Rink

Arkansas Skatium Roller Rink

Playtime Pizza

Play Tubes at Rock Creek

Public Libraries

What to expect...

The Central Arkansas region has so many public libraries that there is sure to be one close to you. Each of the libraries offers unique programs, and many of these are catered to children. You can sign up to receive monthly e-mails from CALS (Central Arkansas Library System) which alert you to every activity program. One of my favorites, Book Babies, is a fun learning time for little ones and their parents, when they sing songs together, read short books, and participate in play time. There are story times for all a arts and crafts, after school activities, reading clubs, music and movement, and so much more! When children are young, you have a great opportunity to show them that libraries can be fun and exciting. of the best things you can do is to encourage your children to fall in love with reading!

In the chart below, you will find the libraries and addresses as listed on the *Central Arkansas Library System* website. You can find more information about each library by visiting the website at: *http://www.cals.lib.ar.us/about/locations.aspx*.

Main Library	100 Rock Street Little Rock, AR 72201
Dee Brown	6325 Baseline Road Little Rock, AR 72209
John Gould Fletcher	823 North Buchanan Street Little Rock, AR 72205
Maumelle	10 Lake Pointe Drive Maumelle, AR 72113
Sidney S. McMath	2100 John Barrow Road Little Rock, AR 72204
Max Milam	609 Aplin Avenue Perryville, AR 72126
Esther Dewitt Nixon	703 W. Main Street Jacksonville, AR 72076
Oley E. Rooker	11 Otter Creek Court Little Rock, AR 72210
Amy Sanders	31 Shelby Drive Sherwood, AR 72120
Adolphine Fletcher Terry	2015 Napa Valley Drive Little Rock, AR 72212
Roosevelt Thompson	38 Rahling Circle Little Rock, AR 72223
Sue Cowan Williams	1800 Chester Street Little Rock, AR 72206
Cox Creative Center	120 River Market Avenue Little Rock, AR 72201
Butler Center for Arkansas Studies	401 President Clinton Avenue Little Rock, AR 72201

5

Getting Wet, Staying Cool

ack up a bag—sunscreen, drinks, snacks and towels—and get ready to make a big plash! Arkansas offers many places to get wet and have a great time. Remember hat splash parks are very popular, thus arriving early means you'll have fewer rowds to battle.

Courtesy of Emily Benton Ryan

Buffalo National River

What to expect...

The Buffalo National River, , established in 1972, is America's first national river. This beautiful, wild river flows uninhibited for 135 winding miles through the Ozarks to its confluence with the White River. Towering bluffs, a large cave system, beaches, lush forests, and 22 river access points make this a national treasure.

Although access to the river is open all year, the best time to go rafting, kayaking, swimming, or canoeing is during the spring and early summer before the water level gets too low. Many liveries are located along the highways, offering canoe, raft, and kayak rentals.

Lodging, including cabins and camp sites, are located along the river. Make sure that you reference the park service website when planning your trip. You're sure to make unforgettable memories!

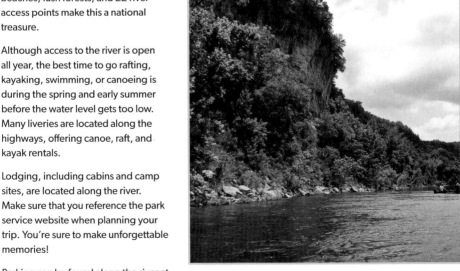

Parking can be found along the river at lodging sites, camp sites, or at canoe/raft/kayak rental stores.

For more information about the park, you can visit the National Park Service website at *www.nps.gov/buff/* or call (870) 439-2502.

Magic Springs & Crystal Falls

1701 East Grand Avenue
Hot Springs, 71901
(501) 624–0100
www.magicsprings.com

Hours:
Magic Springs & Crystal Falls has different hours every month it's open, April - October. Check the park's website, under "Plan a Visit/Calendar" for a full listing.

Admission:
Age 0-3: Free; Age 4-54: $45.00.

Parking:
Parking is $10.00 per vehicle.

Food:
No outside food or drink allowed, with the exception of every Sunday in June. On "Cooler Sundays," you may bring a cooler, but you may not bring any glass or alcoholic beverages.

Discounts:
Age 55+: $29.99; Children 48" and under: $30.00; Active military and public service persons: $15.00 with ID. Memorial Day Weekend: Free for active/retired military w/ID.

What to expect...

Magic Springs & Crystal Falls is Arkansas' premiere water and theme park. If you're planning a trip here, make sure that you carve out an entire day for this fun-filled park!

In the water park, you must wear a bathing suit; suits with any buckles, zippers, or metal are prohibited. Outside the water park, shirts, shorts, and shoes must be worn to ride attractions. You may not bring your own flotation devices. Life jackets for small children are available at the tube distribution area for free.

You must be at least 36" to ride most of the kids' rides, which include: Fearless Flyers, Looney Ballooney, Bugga Booga Wheel, Kit n' Kaboodle Express, Li'l Leapin' Lizards, Clown Around, and Krazy Cars. Plenty of family rides are available as well: Diamond Mine Coaster, Rum Runner Pirate Ship, Twist n' Shout, Carousel, and Razorback Roundup.

The Wading Pool and Bear Cub Bend are perfect for little ones. Both feature a wading pool and water activities that are appropriate for small children.

The Park offers the following dining options: Edy's Ice Cream Parlor, Blue Canoe, Deep Woods Diner, Dippin' Dots, Funnel Cake, Goodie Gallery, Ouachita Mountain Barbeque Company, Pizza Di Lago, Susie Q's Famous Pretzels, Split Rock Grill, Terrace Treats, Timberline Potato Company, Slush Puppy Station, and Incredible Edibles. You'll have no trouble finding delicious food here! Magic Springs & Crystal Falls hosts well-known entertainers throughout the year. Check the schedule in advance, and you can combine fun with live entertainment.

The park offers the following shopping options: Plaza Emporium, Auntie May's Candy Store, Surf Shop, Flip Your Lid Hat Shop, Simply Christian, Old Time Photos, and Magic Ink, Inc. Restrooms are located throughout the park, with changing tables. The park has three ATMs located near the front gate, Auntie May's Candy Store, and the entrance to Timberwood Amphitheater. Make sure to grab a map when you enter the park or print one off the website ahead of time.

Annual Events...

Picnic in the Park, first Sunday in September from 2:00 - 4:00. Enjoy fried chicken, baked beans, corn on the cob, cole slaw, buttermilk biscuits, and blackberry cobbler.

Magic Screams, weekends in October.

Peabody Park

Hours:
8:00 AM - 10:00 PM, daily

Parking:
Parking in the River Market District.

Food:
You may bring your own food and drink. Benches and a covered pavilion are available.

202 East LaHarpe Boulevard
Little Rock, 72201

What to expect...

How do I put this? Peabody Park is SO MUCH FUN!

Could you hear me shouting? I really love this park, and it's very easy to keep an eye on your children. The splash park is completely open with benches all around. If you get there early, you can nearly have the park to yourself. (In case you have trouble figuring out how to turn on the water like I did, just rub your hand over one of the dark discs located throughout.)

The park also offers tunnels, a long tube slide, a tree room, a climbing wall, and other activity areas. This park is located right next to Riverfront Park and just behind the River Market building, and offers plentiful green space, and a view of the beautiful Arkansas River.

The best place to park is by the River Market Pavilion; parking costs $5.00, but it's right on the edge of the park. Benches are scattered all over Peabody Park and the Ozark Pavilion overlooks most of the park as well as the Arkansas River, providing a gorgeous vistas and a perfect place to eat lunch or a snack.

Just Around the Corner...

Old State House Museum

Museum of Discovery

Riverfront Park

War Memorial Park

Hours:
Sunrise - 10:00 PM

Admission:
FREE!

Parking:
Free parking lot.

Food:
You may bring your own food and drink. Picnic tables and benches are available.

5101 West Markham Street
Little Rock, 72205
(501) 371 - 4770
www.littlerock.org/parksrecreation

Getting Wet, Staying Cool

What to expect...

From trails and swings to a brand-new splash park complete with hidden tunnels, War Memorial Park Playground is sure to be a favorite for your little ones! Plenty of shaded areas, covered picnic tables, and wide lawn spaces with enormous trees make this an idyllic spot for picnics and playdates.

The splash park is the main attraction. Make sure that your kids wear shoes that can get wet. The splash park is comprised of tunnels, slides and a rope web. Water bursts from behind every rock, which make up most of the splash park (so parents might want to wear something that can get wet, too). As the rocks can be slippery, parents will want to supervise the little ones.

A lovely playground area with several swings, an angled climbing tree, covered picnic tables, and restrooms with changing tables can be found on the other side of the splash park.

Budget ample time to enjoy this flively park. Your children are sure to love it, and you're sure to come back!

Remember to pack sunscreen!

Just Around the Corner...

All Aboard Restaurant and Grill

Little Rock Zoo

The Painted Pig

Wild River Country

Hours:
10:00 AM - 8:00 PM, Monday - Saturday
12:00 PM - 8:00 PM, Sunday

Admission:
Age 0-2: Free; Age 3-12: $20.99; Age 13-59: $29.99;
Age 60+: $10.99

Parking:
Free parking lot.

Food:
No outside food or drink allowed.

6820 Crystal Hill Road
North Little Rock, 72118
(501) 753 - 8600
www.wildrivercountry.com

What to expect...

Go ahead and spend the entire day at Wild River Country because your children are never going to want to leave! The water park is the largest in Arkansas, with the largest wave pool in the state. It gets very crowded in the summer; the best time to avoid crowds is when the park opens.

The Cyclone, Pipeline, Sidewinder, and Accelerator are rides you can enjoy with your child, sharing a large raft or connected tubes. Vertigo, Vortex, Black Lightning, and White Lightning are one-at-a-time individual slides. The Lazy River, River Rapids, Wave Pool, and Tad Pool (a designated toddler play area) are perfect for younger children.

Picnic tables and vendors located throughout the park make staying for lunch or dinner simple. Lockers are available at an additional fee, if you don't want to carry a bag.

The park is open from late May to early September. Check the website for specific dates. Restrooms with changing tables are located around the park.

Just Around the Corner...

Big Dam Bridge

Burns Park

The Old Mill

The Great Outdoors

There's no doubt about it: Arkansas is a beautiful state. With rivers, mountains, and lots of wide open spaces, Arkansas offers the perfect opportunity to get outdoors and explore. The state parks each have unique vistas, trails, and activities. Make sure to tour the visitor centers before exploring the parks. One of the best things you can do for children is to let them play outdoors!

Courtesy of Emily Benton Ryan

Allsopp Park

Hours:
Sunrise - 10:00 PM, daily

Admission:
FREE!

Parking:
Free parking lot.

Food:
You may bring your own food and drink. Picnic tables and benches are available.

3700 Cedar Hill Road
Little Rock, 72201
(501) 371 - 4770
www.littlerock.org/ParksRecreation/parks/

What to expect...

With mountain biking trails, paved trails, tennis courts, a pavilion, a ballpark, a playground, and vast open space, Allsop Park is one of Little Rock's most popular parks, and is great for birthday parties, playdates, or picnics.

The baseball field provides a spot to play a game of kickball or to bring gloves and play catch. Woods surround the park, and the playground area is nearly completely shaded—an ideal place for bringing little ones and for enjoying lunch together.

The paved trails throughout the park are all fairly short. The trail located at the back of the park goes through the woods at a steady incline. It's a good workout—especially if you're pushing a stroller!

There are portable restrooms by the playground as well as permanent restrooms by the baseball field. The park is located off of Cantrell Road, so many yummy restaurant options can be found if you didn't pack a lunch.

Just Around the Corner...

Murray Park

The Painted Pig

River Market District

Big Dam Bridge

Hours:
The Bridge is always open, unless noted under "Closures" on the website.

Admission:
FREE!

Parking:
Free parking lots.

Food:
You may bring your own food and drink. Benches are available on and by the bridge.

What to expect...

Little Rock side:
7600 Rebsamen Park Road
Little Rock, 72207

North Little Rock side:
4000 Cooks Landing Road
North Little Rock, 72118
(501) 340 - 6800
www.bigdambridge.com

With 3 million pounds of steel, 24 million pounds of concrete, 679 feet of walled embankment, and 4,226 linear feet of bridge, the Big Dam Bridge lives up to its name. The bridge was opened in September 2006, and has become a favorite destination of locals and visitors alike. Between the grandeur of the bridge and the breathtaking views, it's where just about everyone wants to exercise.

The bridge's moniker stems from the fact that the bridge is also a dam. When the dam is open, it's thrilling to watch the waters of the Arkansas River come ripping and churning through. For those of you who might be uncomfortable with heights, you might want to try out the Two Rivers Bridge instead.

This is a great place to put your child in the stroller and get some exercise. The cool breeze coming from the Arkansas River, coupled with the gorgeous views, will inspire you to keep pushing forward, and your child is sure to be mesmerized by the scenery that wraps around you!

On the North Little Rock side of the Bridge, there is a permanent restroom facility. On the Little Rock side, there are portable restrooms.

Just Around the Corner...

Burns Park

Murray Park

Two Rivers Park

Blanchard Springs Caverns

NF 54, Forest Road 1110A
Fifty-Six, 72533
(870) 757 - 2211
www.fs.usda.gov/osfnf

Hours:
9:30 AM - 6:00 PM, daily from mid-March through October
9:30 AM - 6:00 PM, Wednesday - Sunday from November through mid-March
10:30 AM - 4:30 PM, daily tours

Admission:
Age 0-5: Free; Age 6-15: $5.00 for Dripstone/Discovery tours; Age 16-61: $10.00 for Dripstone/Discovery tours; Age 62+: $5.00 for Dripstone/Discovery tours; Wild Cave Tour: $75.00 per person

Parking:
Free parking lot.

Food:
No outside food or drink allowed.

What to expect...

Surrounded by the lush Ozark National Forest, Blanchard Springs Caverns is a sight to behold. Your children must see the inexplicable beauty of these formations. The Blanchard Springs Caverns get their name from a gushing spring at the base of the mountain. Entering this underground world is a thrilling experience for both adults and children. When the miserably hot Arkansas summers are upon us, what better way to beat the heat than in the cool 58-degree climate underground?

Three different tours are offered: the Dripstone Trail, the Discovery Trail, and the Wild Cave Tour. On all tours, it's a good idea to bring a light jacket and shoes with good traction. Make sure that you use the restroom before embarking. There is a changing table in the women's restroom.

I highly recommend the Dripstone Trail tours, which expose you to the most formations, and are available year-round. This one-hour tour is very easy and you can even push a stroller on the paved walkways. The tour covers 4/10 of a mile, with two seating areas available. Stairs are encountered at one point, but they can be avoided.

The Discovery Trail, more difficult than the Dripstone Trail, requires an hour and a half, and contains approximately 700 stair steps. This trail makes its way through the lower portion of the caverns. The Discovery Trail tours are open from June through August.

Lasting for 3-4 hours, the Wild Cave Tour explores the undeveloped sections in the middle level of the caverns. Don't go on this trail unless you are ready to get dirty! On parts of this tour, you will crawl on your hands and knees, pass under low ceilings, and climb steep slopes. Caving equipment will be provided. You must be at least ten years old to participate, and an adult must accompany children ages 10-12. The Wild Cave Tour is available by reservation only, April through October.

Burns Park

Hours:
6:00 AM - 12:00 AM, daily

Admission:
FREE!

Parking:
Free parking lots.

Food:
You may bring your own food and drink. Picnic tables and benches are available

Interstate 40, Exit 150
North Little Rock, 72118
(501) 791 - 8538
www.nlrpr.org

What to expect...

Spanning 1,700 acres, Burns Park offers a host of activities for children and adults alike. With an antebellum cabin, covered bridge, fishing pier, playgrounds, 27 tennis courts, camping areas, two 18-hole golf courses, 17 soccer fields, batting cages, softball/baseball fields, hiking and paved trails, a seasonal amusement park, and a 3-acre dog park, there is more than enough to do!

You can easily spend an entire day of fun at Burns Park.
Several pavilions, picnic areas, and benches provide lunch spots. The playgrounds and trails are my favorite parts of the park. The trails span miles and are mostly paved, so bring your stroller. One of the trails connects with the Big Dam Bridge and is part of the River Trail. The Holiday Lights Festival is a spectacular event featuring over 50 holiday light displays!

Contact the park to find out when the amusement park opens. To make reservations for tennis or golf, contact the administrative office. Burns Park is a beautiful, spacious park that provides fun for the entire family!

Just Around the Corner...

Big Dam Bridge

Millennium Bowl

Wild River Country

Devil's Den State Park

Hours:
Visitor Center: 8:00 AM - 5:00 PM, daily
Admission:
FREE!
Parking:
Free parking lots.
Food:
You may bring your own food and drink. Picnic tables and benches are available.

11333 West Arkansas Highway 74
West Fork, 72774
(479) 761 - 3325
www.arkansasstateparks.com/devilsden/

What to expect...

Come enjoy the beauty of one of Arkansas' most breathtaking state parks complete with waterfalls, trails, streams, caves, and a plethora of outdoor activities. Devil's Den State Park offers cabins, and if you're going to make the drive from Little Rock, I would recommend staying for more than just one day. This state park offers much to be seen and much to do for the entire family.

Lake Trail, a half-mile in length, is an easy, enjoyable hike that meanders alongside Lee Creek and leads to the spectacular dam which creates Lake Devil.

Devil's Den Self-Guided Trail, 1.5 miles in length, is a beautiful trail that journeys past waterfalls, lush forest terrain, and peaceful springs.

Fossil Flats, 5 miles in length, gets its name from the fossil formations in the exposed creek bed. Big rock formations as well as evidence of early settlers can be seen along this trail.

Gorley King, 7 miles in length, is perhaps too long for little ones. You can, however, hike some of it and enjoy the scenery—beautiful cedar glades, natural bridges, and a breathtaking view of the Dam and Lake Devil.

For the trails, I would recommend a baby carrier for little ones. A restaurant, boat rental, pool, and park store add to the enjoyment. Call in advance and make a reservation if you're planning an overnight stay. It's also wise to check the seasonal hours of the park's various amenities.

Garvan Woodland Gardens

550 Arkridge Road
Hot Springs National Park, 71913
(501) 262 - 9300
www.garvangardens.com

Hours:
9:00 AM - 6:00 PM, daily, February through mid-November
12:00 PM - 9:00 PM, daily, mid-November through December
The gardens are closed on Thanksgiving, Christmas, and New Year's.

Admission:
Age 0-5: Free; Age 6-12: $5.00; Age 13-54: $10.00; Age 55+: $9.00

Parking:
Free parking lot.

Food:
You may bring your own food and drink, but no coolers. Benches are available.

What to expect...

Garvan Woodland Gardens offers nearly unmatched beauty. Tulips, Japanese maples, daffodils, weeping willows, splashing waterfalls, and crystal streams conjure a sense of tranquility as you walk over intricate, unique bridges and along paths through the seemingly-endless gardens. If you're looking for a place to teach your children about the beauty of nature, it doesn't get much more picturesque than this.

The best times of year to go to the Gardens are when the tulips and daffodils are blooming in March and April, and during the holiday lights display from November to December. The springtime flowers are a sight to see. Here, you will find nearly every type of tulip in fields that stretch into eternity. The first time I came to Garvan Woodland Gardens, I couldn't believe how majestic it was.

If you decide to see the holiday lights, the rule is: the earlier, the better. The lights are turned on at 5:00 PM, and if you show up after that, you might be waiting in your car for a while (so make sure to pack some snacks and entertainment). During the holiday lights display, they serve hot chocolate and snacks. If you have little ones, bring a stroller because the pathways through the gardens are extensive.

Anthony Chapel is a beautiful place to take your children. Nestled in the woods and camouflaged by the forest, this is one of the architectural jewels of the state. If you are visiting the gardens on a Saturday, call ahead and make sure that there are no weddings because if there are, you won't be able to see the chapel.

The women's restroom, located inside the welcome center, has a changing table. The Garvan Woodland Gardens gift shop offers a wide variety of beautiful gifts.

Hobbs State Park

20201 Arkansas Highway 12
Rogers, 72756
(479) 789-5000
www.FriendsofHobbs.com

Hours:
The Visitor Center is open from 8:00 AM - 5:00 PM, daily. The trailheads close half an hour after sundown.

Admission:
The park and the Visitor Center are free!

Workshops do cost a small fee, register at the visitor center. Visit the park's website to find out about these activities.

Parking:
Free parking lots.

Food:
Outside food and drink are not allowed in the Visitor's Center.

Picnic tables and benches are available.

What to expect...

Walking into the visitor center creates the feeling of walking into a tree house. High ceilings with tall windows expose lush foliage that circles the building. The children's corner is the perfect place for toddlers to play rambunctiously on the floor with an enormous puzzle, books, magazines, and stuffed animals. The center houses an exhibit which displays the history of the Peter Van Winkle industrial mill complex, antebellum home, and slave quarters; a butterfly exhibit; a bat exhibit with a giant, plastic bat that allows kids an up-close look; and, perhaps the most interesting of all, an intricate cave exhibit that is set up to look like an actual cave. As children enter the cave, they can press buttons and watch as salamanders, cave crickets, bats, stalagmites and stalactites light up in the darkness. An observation station overlooking the woods and a small pond beckon children to reach for the binoculars and observe the birds and wildlife. Restrooms with changing tables and water fountains are available. Pets are not allowed inside.

The visitor center also offers over 1,500 educational programs throughout the year, engaging children of all ages. Various activities take place daily, such as scavenger hunts, discovery cruises, eagle watching tours, reading time, and engaging guest lectures. To find out what activities are going on, visit the park's website.

Ozark Plateau, Sinking Streams, and Historic Van Winkle are three easier hikes suitable for children. The first of these trails, the Ozark Plateau, is located at the visitor center. This trail is a quarter-mile long, and completely paved, so pushing a stroller would be easy. Several benches along the trail allow visitors to stop and enjoy the peace of the dense forest. The second trail, Sinking Streams, meanders along a creek and down into beautiful terrain completing a half-mile loop. Although most of the trail is easy, a fairly narrow steep section isn't passable with a stroller, making this hike best for kids three years and up. The final trail is the Historic Van Winkle Trail. This is a flat crushed gravel half-mile loop suitable for jogging strollers. The historic markers and remains of the mill make this trail interesting and educational. The trailhead for both the Sinking Streams and Historic Van Winkle trails trails is just off of Highway 12, and has a parking lot with restrooms, a picnic table, and water fountains.

Lake Willastein Park

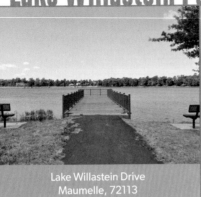

Hours:
Sunrise to sunset, daily.

Admission:
FREE!

Parking:
Free parking lot.

Food:
You may bring your own food and drink. Picnic tables and benches are available.

Lake Willastein Drive
Maumelle, 72113
(501) 851 - 6990
maumelleparksandrec.com/PARKS.html

What to expect...

Lake Willastein is one of my favorite parks. You can easily spend hours there, enjoying all the park has to offer. The lake, usually inhabited by ducks, geese, turtles, and the occasional fisherman, is beautiful. The park is typically cooler with a breeze coming off the lake.

One of my favorite aspects of this park are the paved walking trails that wind around the park and lake. The park's website has maps for each trail, providing direction and information on the length. Your little one is sure to get excited about spotting some turtles or ducks. You could easily push the stroller for an hour of exercise.

Lake Willastein Park has two playground areas and two swing sets—mostly in the shade so you don't need to worry about your children getting a sunburn. The playground is located beside a very nice restroom facility with a changing table in the women's room. There are benches all around, and the woods provide the perfect backdrop to the play area.

With large trees that stretch shade over soft grass, it would be a shame not to pack a picnic. Lake Willastein is so beautiful and relaxing that you will be glad you stretched out that big ol' quilt and brought some lunches. If you're wondering what those big bunkers are, they were built in 1942 for storing military munitions during World War II!

My GPS doesn't bring up Lake Willastein Park. In case you aren't sure where to turn, make sure that you take a left before Kroger onto Odom Boulevard, and then take your first right behind Kroger. You will see the lake and the park off to the left.

Annual Events. . .

Fourth Fest, on July 4th, includes food, crafts, music, and a fireworks display.

Just Around the Corner...

Big Dam Bridge

Jump Zone

Millennium Bowl

Mt. Magazine State Park

16878 Highway 309 South
Paris, 72855
(479) 963 - 8502
www.mountmagazinestatepark.com

Hours:
Sunrise to sunset, daily.

Admission:
FREE!

Parking:
Free parking lots.

Food:
You may bring your own food and drink. A few picnic tables are located at the campground/picnic area. The Skycrest Restaurant is located inside the Lodge at Mt. Magazine.

What to expect...

Mount Magazine is the highest point in Arkansas and boasts views you'll be hard-pressed to find anywhere else in the state. The rustic Lodge at Mt. Magazine is a wonderful place to stay. The gift shop, pool, restaurant, and easily-accessible trails are great for the entire family. If you choose to stay at Mt. Magazine, you can also rent a cabin or stay at the campground.

Be aware that the Mt. Magazine District of the Ozark National Forest has one of the state's highest bear populations. The park's website has a page devoted to bear safety that you should read before visiting the park.

The two trails described as "easy" hikes are Benefield Loop Trail (2 miles) and Will Apple's Road Trail (1.6 miles). Bear Hollow Trail (2.8 miles), the Mossback Ridge Trail (2.1 miles), and Signal Hill Trail (1.5 miles) are all "moderate" trails and offer spectacular views and interesting sights. Signal Hill is the highest point in Arkansas, with an elevation of 2,753 feet above sea level. Since most of the trails are rocky, I recommend bringing a child carrier for infants and toddlers. If you have older children, you might be interested in the three-hour or five-hour ATV guided tours along Huckleberry Mountain Trail.

Make sure that you visit the lodge and the visitor center. Both describe the history of the park, provide educational materials, and feature friendly staff who are eager to ensure that your family makes the most of their visit.

Murray Park

Hours:
Sunrise - 10:00 PM, daily.

Admission:
FREE!

Parking:
Free parking lots.

Food:
You may bring your own food and drink. Picnic tables and benches are available.

4301 Rebsamen Park Drive
Little Rock, 72202
(501) 371 - 4770
www.littlerock.org/ParksRecreation/

What to expect...

Located beside the Arkansas River, Murray Park is unquestionably one of the city's most popular parks. With downtown, the River Trail, Burns Park, the Big Dam Bridge, Rebsamen Park Golf Course, and Two Rivers Park in close proximity, Murray Park is always full of people—playing a game of soccer or sand volleyball, jogging, fishing, biking, playing on the playground, or enjoying a picnic.

The park has eight pavilions which are available to rent. Three soccer fields, sand volleyball courts, a boat dock, a dog park, and two playgrounds (one handicap accessible) are part of this enormously fun park. The playgrounds are large and are perfect for children of all ages.

Murray Park is home to Paws Park—the city's first fenced-in, off-leash dog park. It's the ideal place to bring your dog and let her roam around. After the children and the dog have exhausted all their energy, you can enjoy lunch and the beautiful scenery of the Arkansas River.

Just Around the Corner...

Big Dam Bridge

Burns Park

Two Rivers Park

The Old Mill

Fairway Avenue and Lakeshore Drive
North Little Rock, 72116
(501) 758 - 1424

Hours:
Sunrise - sunset, daily.

Admission:
FREE!

Parking:
Free parking along the street.

Food:
You may bring your own food and drink. Picnic tables and benches are available.

What to expect...

"My first visit to The Old Mill is one of my earliest childhood memories. It seemed then that it was a place graced by magic and all these years later, it still seems that way to me. I urge anyone visiting our beautiful city to make it a must do on your sightseeing list. You'll never see anything quite like it."

—Mary Steenburgen, Academy Award winning actress

The Old Mill, which is listed on the National Register of Historical Places, is one of my favorite places to enjoy a picnic and take family photographs. On a spring day, the cherry blossoms,

gristmill, lake, woods, and fountain provide a gorgeous backdrop. It is no small wonder that the mill's claim to fame is its inclusion in the opening scenes of *Gone with the Wind*. Historic in its own right, the mill was completed in 1933, and the first floor of the gristmill dates back to 1828. The mill is located in the T. R. Pugh Memorial Park at the corner of Fairway Avenue and Lakeshore Drive.

Tables, benches, a small amphitheater, and open grassy areas allow visitors to bring a lunch and enjoy the scenery. A pathway leads to the lake, which has become a part of the residential community around the mill. Visitors can go inside the mill, and explore the bare floors and open windows, and get a great view of the churning water. A stairway inside the small interior of the mill makes using a stroller nearly impossible. Guided tours are available with reservations and typically last for thirty minutes.

Just Around the Corner...

Burns Park

River Market District

Wild River Country

The Great Outdoors

Petit Jean

1285 Petit Jean Mountain Road
Morrilton, 72110
(501) 727 - 5441
www.petitjeanstatepark.com

Hours:
The Park is open year-round and the visitor center is open from 8:00 AM - 5:00 PM, daily.
Admission:
FREE!

Parking:
Free parking lots.

Food:
You may bring your own food and drink. Picnic tables and benches are available.

What to expect...

Petit Jean, Arkansas' oldest state park, is a must. You can easily spend a whole day in the park hiking, exploring, and enjoying all the sights and activities that Petit Jean has to offer.

While there are no paved trails, a few trails are perfect for younger children. My favorite trail in the park is Bear Cave Trail. Towering, unique rock formations and a few caves make this quarter-of-a-mile trail exciting and adventurous. The trail got its name because the last bear in Petit Jean was killed along its path. Canyon Trail and Rock House Cave Trail are also great hikes with children. Rock House Cave Trail is the state's premiere spot for viewing Native American rock art (estimated to be over 500 years old)!

Another fun locale is the Cedar Falls overlook. If you don't want to make the two-mile hike (deemed "strenuous" by the Park because of its steepness) down to the bottom of the falls, this overlook offers a spectacular view of the waterfall and the surrounding cliffs and forest. Petit Jean's gravesite is another great place to appreciate a stunning vista. You can look out over stretching farmland, undulating hills, and the Arkansas River. Finally, the view from Mather Lodge will make you aware that you are hemmed in by staggering cliffs and lush foliage. You will be glad you took your children to these three overlooks, which happen to be located close to each other.

Petit Jean State Park offers nice, clean camping sites. A gift shop, located in Mather Lodge, offers unique trinkets that go beyond your typical state park sweatshirts and mugs. Mather Lodge also houses a restaurant. Tennis courts, a swimming pool, cabins, a wide variety of programs and tours, and even the state's Automobile Museum are all parts of this amazing park that will leave you with priceless family memories.

Pinnacle Mountain State Park

Hours:
6:30 AM - one hour after sunset, daily. The visitor center is open from 8:00 AM - 5:00 PM, daily.

Admission:
FREE!

Parking:
Free parking lots.

Food:
You may bring your own food and drink. Picnic tables and benches are available.

11901 Pinnacle Valley Road
Little Rock, 72223
(501) 868-5806

What to expect...

Pinnacle Mountain State Park is one of my favorite places to bring my children and to meet up with friends for playdates. The main park area has a huge, open field that is perfect for spreading out picnic blankets, running around with bare feet, and throwing a frisbee. Recently, the playground area was completely redone, and the new

playground is one of the best in the city.

The park is gorgeous and the mountain quietly adds a surreal beauty to the natural landscape. Two trails, the Kingfisher Trail (half-mile) and the Arkansas Trail in the Arkansas Arboretum (.6 mile) are both paved and wind through beautiful forests and by rushing streams. These trails are perfect for engaging children's curiosity in nature, which will be further fueled with a trip to the visitor center. My son could run around the visitor center for hours going back and forth between the enormous live bee colony, the observation station, the creature room with snakes, turtles, spiders, and a baby alligator, and the hands-on exploration table with antlers, fossils, a turtle shell, and much more.

Other than the two paved trails, none of the other trails in the park are stroller-friendly. I would recommend bringing a child carrier for little ones. The mountain is a fun challenge, but if you have young children with you make sure that you climb the west side. You will want to stay away from the east side, which could be dangerous for children. If your child is old enough to enjoy hiking, then she is old enough to make it up Pinnacle. It is 1 ½ miles up and down the mountain, and there are plenty of places along the way to stop for a water break and to take in the gorgeous, one-of-a-kind views. The view from the top is well worth the hike!

The park offers a wide variety of programs and activities year-round. For more information, visit the *State Parks of Arkansas* website at *www.arkansasstateparks.com/pinnaclemountain/* .

Riverfront Park

Hours:
8:00 AM - 10:00 PM, daily.

Admission:
FREE!

Parking:
Parking in the River Market District.

Food:
You may bring your own food and drink.

LaHarpe Boulevard
Little Rock, 72201
(501) 375 - 2552

What to expect...

Stretching 11 blocks along the south bank of the Arkansas River, Riverfront Park is a spectacular place to bring a blanket and enjoy a picnic while soaking in the natural beauty and the vibrant energy of downtown. This park is the location for Movies in the Park, Riverfest, and many other events.

Riverfront Park is located directly behind the River Market building and extends all the way to the Old State House Museum. If you don't have time to pack a lunch, you can run inside the River Market building and grab a bite to eat. Afterward, walk along the river, and check out all the fun things around Riverfront Park.

The Riverfest Amphitheater is located in Riverfront Park and is the location for many summer concerts as well as Movies in the Park. The Medical Mile is a trail designed to inspire healthy living choices. Junction Bridge, also located in the park, is an exceptional location from which to see the Arkansas River. Make sure to check out the History Pavilion and Le Petite Roche Plaza to learn about Little Rock's history!

Just Around the Corner...

Peabody Park

River Rail

Witt Stephens Jr. Central Arkansas Nature Center

Toltec Mounds Archeological State Park

Hours:
8:00 AM - 5:00 PM, Tuesday - Saturday
1:00 PM - 5:00 PM, Sunday

Admission:
FREE!

Parking:
Free parking lot.

Food:
You may bring your own food and drink.

490 Toltec Mounds Road
Scott, 72142
(501) 961 - 9442

What to expect...

At the national historic site of Toltec Mounds Archeological State Park, you'll find the tallest Native American mounds in the state, remanants of a complex which was populated from 650-1050 AD. Only three mounds remain where 18 once stood.

Two stroller-friendly trails (a .75-mile trail and a 1.6 mile trail) are great for children. You can take a guided tour if you call in advance and make a reservation. The archaeological site tour by tram is free for children ages 0-5, $4.00 for children ages 6-12, $5.00 for adults, and $18.00 for a family. The guided walking tour is free for children ages 0-5, $2.00 for children ages 6-12, $3.00 for adults, and $10.00 for a family.

With its location adjacent to Mound Lake, the flat delta landscape—punctuated by the enormous Toltec Mounds—carries a deeply majestic feel. The visitor center features artifacts from the site, a theater, and an archeological research laboratory. A great place to eat a picnic lunch, a fun visitor center to explore, and easy walking trails make this state park a perfect one to bring little ones!

For more information, you can visit the *State Parks of Arkansas* website at www.arkansasstateparks.com/toltecmounds.

Just Around the Corner...

Plantation Agriculture Museum

Two Rivers Park

Hours:
Sunrise - sunset, daily.

Admission:
FREE!

Parking:
Free parking lots.

Food:
You may bring your own food and drink. Benches are available.

From the Park:	**From the Bridge:**
County Farm Road	6900 Two Rivers Road
Little Rock, 72223	Little Rock, 72211
	(501) 371 - 4770

What to expect. . .

Two Rivers Park is perhaps my favorite place in Little Rock to push the stroller and get some exercise. Because it is located along the Arkansas River, all of the trails in the park are perfectly flat—great for biking and a tired momma pushing a bulky double stroller.

The park is close to the Big Dam Bridge which connects with Burns Park, so if you want to go for a long family bike ride, you can easily put many miles under your tires. My favorite trail at Two Rivers Park winds through pristine pine forests, a swamp, and rolling grasslands and leads to the Two Rivers Park Bridge—a sight not to be missed! The walking bridge allows the view of the Arkansas River, the Big Dam Bridge, and the Interstate 430 bridge.

Two Rivers Park is home to the Pulaski County public garden, where you can share your green thumb and love of gardening with your children. The park has restrooms.

Just Around the Corner...

Big Dam Bridge

Burns Park

Pinnacle Mountain State Park

Wildwood Park for the Arts

Hours:
9:00 AM - 5:00 PM, Monday - Friday; 10:00 AM - 5:00 PM, Saturday; 12:00 PM - 5:00 PM, Sunday.

Admission:
FREE!

Parking:
Free parking lot.

Food:
You may bring your own food and drink.

20919 Denny Road
Little Rock, 72223
(501) 821 - 7275
www.wildwoodpark.org

What to expect...

Wildwood Park for the Arts is the perfect place to enjoy beautiful weather in an environment where children are free to run around, admire the gardens, and skip rocks on Swan Lake. An idyllic hideaway in Little Rock, Wildwood Park is a peaceful place to have a picnic or to go for a walk.

Several times during the year, events and festivals catered to families take place at Wildwood. For information on upcoming events, visit the website. Educational programs, offered year-round, focus on everything from art to opera and foreign language. During the summer, camps for elementary-aged children focus on arts and humanities.

The gardens at Wildwood Park are expansive and breathtaking. With rushing streams, a thick forest, and colorful blooms, they are worth visiting and admiring. You can schedule a guided garden tour or sign up for a gardening workshop. Many of the paths are paved, making the park stroller-friendly. Throw the picnic blanket in the back of the minivan, load up the kids, and enjoy beautiful scenery.

Just Around the Corner...

Arkansas Skatium Ice Rink

Arkansas Skatium Roller Rink

Barnes & Noble

Pinnacle Mountain State Park

7

Fun on the Farm

Go on a tractor ride! Jump around on hay bales! Pick berries! Cut pumpkins off the vine! If you're ready to get your hands dirty, get some really cute pictures of the kiddos and have a great time, then visit these playdate locations and take advantage of opportunities to teach your children respect for the environment, the value of hard work, and the origins of food! And the best part? There's plenty of space to run around!

Courtesy of Emily Benton Ryan

Bo Brook Farms

13810 Combee Lane
Roland, 72135
(501) 519 - 5666

Hours:
9:00 AM - 5:00 PM, Monday - Friday
9:00 AM - 6:00 PM, Saturday - Sunday

The pumpkin patch and corn maze are open in October.
The blueberries and blackberries grow in May and June.

Parking:
Free parking lot.

Food:
No outside food or drink allowed.

www.bobrookfarms.com www.littlerock.org/ParksRecreation/parks/

What to expect...

Alligators in a swamp, crooked scarecrows scattered about, and witches on brooms (impaled on trees) greet you as you wind down the dirt road to Bo Brook Farms.

Bo Brook Farms is a traditional pumpkin patch, and for this reason, it's the one we go to every year. A small petting zoo awaits as you enter the farm. An enormous corn pit is popular with children—it's big enough that they can run around and enjoy getting messy. Nearby resides a small hay bale maze, designed to be nearly impossible for little ones to get lost in. The hay ride is fun for all ages. The first time I took my oldest on this ride, he was only four-months-old, and he loved it!

My favorite part of Bo Brook is the pumpkin patch— just grab a wheelbarrow and a set of vine cutters, and you're on your way! Take your time and enjoy the lovely fall weather as you meander around the enormous, open field of bright orange pumpkins. Your little ones are sure to enjoy running around, taking turns pushing and riding the wheelbarrow, and picking out pumpkins.

In May and June, Bo Brook Farms has abundant blueberry and blackberry crops. Make sure to arrive early in the morning to avoid the heat. Pre-picked berries cost $4.00 per pint. I recommend picking your own at the discounted price of $2.00 per pint. It's a great deal plus a ton of fun!

There are no changing tables in the restrooms.

Farmers' Market

400 President Clinton Avenue
Little Rock, 72201
501) 375 - 2552
www.rivermarket.info/learn-more/farmers-market.aspx

Hours:
7:00 AM - 3:00 PM, Tuesday and Saturday, late-April
through late-October

Admission:
FREE!

Parking:
Parking is available in the River Market District.

Food:
You may bring your own food and drink. Tables and
benches are available.

What to expect...

The Farmers' Market is located in the River Market District of downtown—an area hopping with music, great food, shops, museums, entertainment, and just about anything that says "local" and "laid back." It is the perfect place to bring children. The Farmers' Market gets busier as the day goes on, thus morning provides respite from crowds. Little restaurants abound inside the River Market building, attached to the Farmers' Market. Bring the stroller, find a table, and enjoy breakfast. The best part? Kids can be really, really loud and nobody cares!

The Farmers' Market is bustling with people grabbing a bite to eat, buying produce, meeting up with friends, and enjoying the fun and relaxed atmosphere. Famers peddle juicy watermelons, vibrant flowers, homemade jam, and just about every fruit and vegetable you could want—at great prices. Vendors also sell handmade jewelry, birdhouses, knit hats and scarves, purses, and much more. With plenty of space between the tables, it is easy to take your time, browse all the selections, and push that big-ole' stroller stuffed with all your neat and tasty purchases.

The Farmers' Market opens to Riverfront Park and a beautiful view of the Arkansas River. Once you finish shopping or browsing, walk down with your children and let them run around and enjoy the nice weather. However, if it's the middle of a summer day, you might want to find a shady spot instead. Indeed, this is a great way to teach your children the value of local farming and healthy eating. You should find at least one farmer who is more than willing to let your brood try a sample of the delectable cantaloupe grown on his land. Did you know that the Arkansas state vegetable and fruit is the South Arkansas Vine Ripe Pink Tomato? Pick some up while you're there!

Just Around the Corner...

Museum of Discovery

Riverfront Park

Witt Stephens Jr. Central Arkansas Nature Center

Heifer International Learning Centers

Hours:
Heifer Village: 9:00 AM - 5:00 PM, Monday - Saturday
Heifer Ranch: By reservation only

Admission:
Heifer Village: FREE!
Heifer Ranch: Rates vary depending on program and group size.

Parking:
Free parking lot.

Food:
No outside food or drink allowed.

Fun on the Farm

What to expect...

Heifer Ranch:	**Heifer Village:**
55 Heifer Road	1 World Avenue
Perryville, 72126	Little Rock, 72202
(501) 907 - 2697	

Heifer International offers two exciting programs for children and adults: Heifer Village in downtown Little Rock and Heifer Ranch in Perryville. Heifer Village provides a hands-on learning experience for children that teaches about solutions to global hunger and poverty. With over 80 interactive exhibits, Heifer Village is a great way to expand your children's minds and make them aware of how they can positively change the world!

Passions are often ignited in youth, and childhood is an opportune time to help children become sensitive and aware of the needs of others. It's empowering to inform a child that he or she can make a difference in the world.

The Café at Heifer, a good lunch spot with kid-friendly options, is open on Monday - Friday from 10:00 AM - 3:00 PM. The shop at Heifer is stocked with Heifer merchandise, educational toys, pottery, and much more! The women's restroom has a changing table.

Heifer Ranch, a learning center and demonstration farm, is an unforgettable experience for parents and elementary or older-aged children who are interested in seeing what a true global village looks like. The global village on display is a collection of homes from around the world in many countries that Heifer serves. Tours and programs give participants a firsthand look at the challenges that come with hunger and poverty. Make reservations two months in advance (501-889-5124). A minimum of seven people per group is required. For more information, you can visit the website at *www.heifer.org* .

Just Around the Corner...

Historic Arkansas Museum

Riverfront Park

William J. Clinton Presidential Library and Museum

Mary's Place

Hours:
9:00 AM - 5:00 PM, Monday - Saturday

Admission:
$5.00 without a pumpkin; $7.50 to pick a pumpkin.

Parking:
Free parking lot.

Food:
You may bring your own food and drink. Picnic tables and benches are available.

3705 Highway 5 North
Bryant, 72022
(501) 847-3900
www.marysplaceinbryant.com

What to expect...

Don't come here looking for the greatest and grandest pumpkin patch in Central Arkansas, Rather, come for a great time with your children, as the focus is not really on the pumpkins. In fact, there aren't many to choose from, but so many other activities are offered that your children are guaranteed to have fun.

The hayride at Mary's Place is the best one I've found. Little towns and graveyards are set up throughout the woods. The ride stops in a town square where you're invited to find your way through a huge maze. Later, you may climb into a tall tree house where you can gaze down on the people wandering through the maze. The hayride is built around the story of Bad Bart, who just escaped from jail and is on the loose. Returning to the hay ride, you'll witness a sudden confrontation between Bad Bart and the sheriff. Parents who do not want their kids to see the confrontation can take a short walk back to the pumpkin patch (I stayed on with my sixteen-month-old and he was fine). After the confrontation, Bad Bart comes up to the hayride, smiles at the children, and lets them know that it was pretend.

There is also a petting zoo with ponies that bite, so make sure you let your kids know. One of my son's favorite parts of Mary's Place was the area for children to ride on miniature John Deere tractors and scooters—all of the children loved this. A bouncy house, a swing set, and a jungle gym round out the attractions, while a covered area full of picnic tables provides the perfect place to enjoy lunch. The nursery and country store are definitely worth checking out. You can pick out some violas and pick up some peanut brittle before you leave! My family had so much fun here. We came for the pumpkins, but left with great memories.

Motley's Tree Farm

13724 Sandy Ann Drive
Little Rock, 72206
(501) 888 - 1129
www.motleystreefarm.com

Hours:
1:00 PM - 5:00 PM, Monday - Friday
9:00 AM - 5:00 PM, Saturday and Sunday

The Tree Farm is open from mid-November through mid-December.

Admission:
FREE!

Parking:
Free parking lot.

Food:
No outside food or drink allowed. Concessions are available by the gift shop.

What to expect...

I can promise you this: your children will not want to leave Motley's Tree Farm! An abundance of kid-centered activities and lots of space to run around make this a fun, family-friendly place to go for your Christmas tree.

Motley's offers a variety of trees, with the option of cutting down your own tree. A tractor ride leads to the Christmas trees, so once you cut it, they can haul it back for you. The pre-cut trees, which include the very popular Fraser fir, are the first ones you see when you enter. These are marked with price tags or reserved tags. Arguably the most popular place to get Christmas trees, Motley's draws large crowds, especially on the weekends and closer to Christmas. The best time to go is when they first open.

The gift shop offers a wide variety of holiday items—anything from stocking holders, snow globes, and ornaments to tree skirts, tree stands, and tree toppers. Motley's sells handmade, fresh wreaths that are one-of-a-kind and less expensive than you'll find elsewhere.

Motley's is stroller-friendly. Although there are no paved areas, the ground is smooth and relatively flat. A petting zoo with several different pens of animals is always swarming with little kids; a hand sanitizing station is located nearby. There are swings with every different sort of seat for little ones. One of the most popular attractions, other than the tractor ride, is the "cow train," a tractor that pulls little buggies with wheels (painted to look like cows) and takes little ones all around the Christmas trees. You have to buy tickets for this separately inside the gift shop. Cash and credit cards are fine, though checks are not accepted. All visitors to Motley's are welcome to a complimentary cup of hot cocoa, available outside the gift shop. The women's restroom has a changing table.

Ozark Folk Center

1032 Park Avenue
Mountain View, 72560
(870) 269 - 3851
www.ozarkfolkcenter.com

Hours:
10:00 AM - 5:00 PM, Tuesday - Saturday

Admission:
Age 0-5: Free; Age 6-12: $8.25 (1 day combination ticket); Age 12+: $17.50; Family Pass: $40.00.

Parking:
Free parking lot.

Food:
No outside food or drink allowed.

What to expect...

The Ozark Folk Center, offering activities for all ages, is an exciting place where history comes to life. With everything being hands-on and kid-friendly, it's a pioneer adventure that your children will not forget! The Folk Center offers three programs, scheduled throughout the year: "Folk Kids," "Young Pioneers," and "Day Camps."

With workshops, pioneer crafts, herb gardens, and plenty of pioneering demonstrations (such as candle making), your children will be engaged in dynamic, educational fun. Crafts include basket weaving, broom making, blacksmithing, pottery making, knife making, weaving, quilting, wood carving, soap making, dress making, herb gardening, doll making, candle making, wood turning, and much more. A ropes course is also located in the state park.

At 7:00 PM, Wednesday through Saturday, your family can enjoy folk music. Since you're in the Ozarks, you're in the perfect part of the country to enjoy the culture and stories that folk music brings. Cabins and a restaurant are available at the state park. Restrooms with changing tables are located at the Folk Center.

Schaefers and Collins Pumpkin Farm

1862 Lollie Road
Mayflower, 72106
(501) 470-3127 and (501) 470-0014
www.schaeferspumpkinpatch.com

Hours:
9:00 AM - 6:00 PM, Monday - Saturday
1:00 PM - 6:00 PM, Sunday

The pumpkin farm is open from late September through October.

Admission:
$5.00 for a hayride and one pumpkin. $1.00 for just a hayride. Cash and checks only.

Parking:
Free parking lot.

Food:
No outside food or drink allowed. Cozy's concession stand offers food and refreshments such as hot dogs, BBQ sandwiches, funnel cakes, shaved ice, and freshly-squeezed lemonade.

What to expect...

Set aside at least an hour and a half for your kids to enjoy this fun pumpkin farm, located a mere 30 minutes by car from Little Rock. Schaefers and Collins Pumpkin Farm is centered on fun activities for children. On weekends, they offer face painting, pony rides, and rock wall climbing.

A fair warning: it's a pumpkin farm, so know that your kids are going to get a little dirty. The site contains swing sets, slides, a bouncy castle, several jungle gyms, and an enormous sandbox. It also features a petting zoo (larger than you might see at a typical pumpkin farm) where children can pet ducks, chickens, pigs, goats, and other cute animals. All of this is spread out in a big, open area, so make sure that you pack sunscreen. Shaded tables and benches abound, in case you want to enjoy some time in the shade.

Most people get their pumpkins by taking the hay ride to the larger pumpkin patch, though a smaller, closer area makes the hayride unnecessary. Here, smaller pumpkins, carving kits, decorative gourds, mums, cornstalks, and small hay bales can be found. Pets are not allowed.

Schaefers Corn Maze

1862 Lollie Road
Mayflower, 72106
(501) 470-3127 and (501) 470-0014
www.schaeferscornmaze.com

Hours:
12:00 PM - 10:30 PM, Friday; 10:00 AM - 10:30 PM, Saturday; 1:00 PM - 8:00 PM, Sunday

The corn maze is opened from early October until October 31st.

Admission:
Age 0-2: Free; Age 3-12: $5.00; Age 13-60: $7.00; 60+: $6.00; Cash or check only.

Parking:
Free parking lot.

Food:
No outside food or drink allowed. A concession stand offers yummy treats like jumbo corndogs, funnel cakes, soft drinks, and shaved ice. Benches are available.

What to expect...

Much more than just a corn maze awaits you when you enter Schaefers Corn Maze. For the little ones, there is face painting, a big jungle gym, and a corn pit surrounded by hay bales. The corn pit and jungle gym are both located in a covered pavilion with plenty of tables and seats. A corn maze express ride is the perfect adventure for children—several cars pulled by an old John Deere tractor meanders through the corn. The ride costs $3.00 and lasts about 10 minutes. Children love it; they think it is exciting to watch the tractor and to get pulled through the corn patch in their own individual riding car.

The smaller kids maze costs $3.00 and is suitable for children five and up to do by themselves. The path is wide and smooth, accomodating a jogging stroller if you want to bring younger kids. The maze takes about 10 minutes, and maps are provided, so you won't get turned around in the corn. The large maze, with an available map, takes 30 to 45 minutes to complete, so make sure you bring something to drink if you embark on this redundant adventure. This maze isn't suitable for young children to do by themselves.

A forty-minute hay ride takes you through Lollie Bottoms and past beautiful farm land, pastures, and the Arkansas River. Adults and kids alike will enjoy this attraction. Just remember to bring sunscreen and expect your little ones to be dirty after all that time in the corn pit, the rides, and the corn maze!

There are portable restrooms with no changing tables.

Creatures Great & Small

8

Children seem to have an innate love of animals. Animals can provide a perfect way to teach your child about being caring and responsible. I would highly recommend getting a family membership to the Little Rock Zoo, as your child will surely want to return over and over again.

Courtesy of Little Rock Zoo

Little Rock Zoo

1 Jonesboro Drive
Little Rock, 72205
(501) 666-2406
www.littlerockzoo.com

Hours:
9:00 AM - 5:00 PM, daily

Last admission is at 4:00 PM.

Admission:
Age 0-12 months: Free; Age 1-12: $8.00; Age 13-59: $10.00; Age 60+: $8.00

Membership:
$85/year for two adults and their children under 18.

Parking:
Parking is $2.00 per vehicle.

Food:
No outside food or drink allowed. Café Africa, located inside the zoo, offers meals, snacks, and refreshments.

What to expect...

The Little Rock Zoo houses 725 animals representing 200 different species. A wide variety of exhibits and activities make the zoo the perfect place to bring children for fun and education. The zoo offers several special exhibits:

Lorikeet Landing is an interactive exhibit where visitors can feed nectar to the lorikeets ($2.00 fee).

Over-the-Jumps Carousel, open on weekends, is an antique carousel near the entrance. It first appeared at the Arkansas State Fair in 1924. The carousel may not operate during fall and winter months. ($2.00 per person).

Penguin Pointe is an outdoor exhibit featuring several different types of penguins.

The train costs $3.00 per person over 12 months of age, and takes you through a shaded part of the zoo at a leisurely pace.

From the giant python to the enormous tiger exhibit, children are sure to have their interests stimulated at the Little Rock Zoo. Plan to spend no less than two hours here if you want to see everything. Strollers and wagons can be rented near the gift shop, although outside strollers and wagons are permitted. Restrooms are located throughout the zoo, all with changing tables. The gift shop is spacious, offering animal-themed gifts, toys, and apparel, as well as snacks and sunscreen.

Annual Events. . .

Breakfast with Animals occurs one morning a month, from March through November.

Boo at the Zoo takes place the last two weeks in October (see next page for details).

Christmas in the Wild is presented during two weekends in December.

Just Around the Corner...

All Aboard Restaurant and Grill

The Painted Pig

Little Rock Central High School National Historic Site

Boo at the Zoo

Hours:
6:00 PM - 9:00 PM.

Boo at the Zoo takes place the last weeks in October. Check the website for exact dates.

Admission:
Age 0-12 months: Free; Age 1+: $7.00; All-inclusive armband: $15.00. Cash only.

Parking:
Free parking lots with shuttle service..

Food:
No outside food or drink allowed, though there are plenty of concession stands inside the zoo.

Discounts:
$1.00 off with advance purchase

Boo at the Zoo Annual Event

Boo at the Zoo is a lively Little Rock tradition and the largest family Halloween festival in Arkansas. This nightly attraction draws huge crowds—some pop in for the haunted house, ghost stories, and haunted walk, while others come to stroll through the zoo at night and see the Halloween lights and decorations. Make sure your children are fully dressed in their Halloween costumes!

Ride on the haunted train, join Frankenstein's dance party, and roast s'mores! An easy-to-complete hay maze beckons children to run around and find the way out. Make sure you bring a flashlight as many corridors are not well lit.

When planning your trip, check the zoo's website to see which special events occur that night. Upon entry, visitors are given a bag to fill with treats from various candy stations. Since Boo at the Zoo is geared for younger children, the bouncy houses, costume contests, carousel rides, magic shows, and ghost stories are sure to leave them excited rather than fearful. Only the haunted house is not geared toward younger children.

With the parking and the big crowds, you should plan to spend at least two hours at Boo at the Zoo. Make sure that you bring extra cash—you'll be glad you did when your five-year-old begs for cotton candy and your two-year-old goes berserk when he sees the line to take a picture with Elmo. Boo at the Zoo is a great way to have fun and get the family in Halloween spirit!

Creatures Great & Small

Witt Stephens Jr. Central Arkansas Nature Center

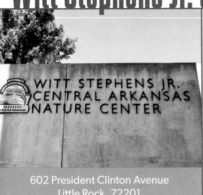

Hours:
8:30 AM - 4:30 PM, Tuesday - Saturday
1:00 PM - 5:00 PM, Sunday.

Admission:
FREE!

Parking:
Parking available in the River Market District.

Food:
No outside food or drink allowed.

602 President Clinton Avenue
Little Rock, 72201
(501) 907 - 0636
www.centralarkansasnaturecenter.com

What to expect...

The Witt Stephens Nature Center is an educational, interactive place where your children will learn about Arkansas wildlife. Located downtown in the heart of the River Market District, the nature center is within walking distance of parks, restaurants, stores, and museums. You could easily make this one stop in a busy day downtown.

Perhaps the most popular feature is an aquarium that spans the length of the main room. Children can observe fish that are

found in five aquatic habitats in Arkansas—a mountain spring, the main channel of a large river, a cypress swamp, a delta marsh, and a bottomland hardwood forest.

A bird-feeding station and the breathtaking view of the Arkansas River make the lounge an intriguing place to explore. Frogs, alligators, and snakes are some of the resident creatures. Every Friday at 2:00 PM they feed the baby alligators—something your children will love to see! The nature center also offers nature stories and activities for children on the second Saturday of each month. The restrooms are connected to the lounge area, adjacent to the center. The women's restroom has a changing table.

"A Bright Future," a 20-minute production about the wildlife and fisheries management of the Arkansas Game and Fish Commission, shows every half-hour starting at 1:30 PM on Sundays and 9:00 AM Tuesday through Saturday.

On your way out, stop by the gift shop and pick up a souvenir. Then, enjoy the gorgeous views all around as you cross the walkway that connects the nature center to the street.

Just Around the Corner...

Museum of Discovery

River Rail

William J. Clinton Presidential Library and Museum

Hodgpodge Fun

This chapter contains descriptions of playdate locations that don't fit neatly into any other category. They are fun, unique, and worthwhile places to visit!

Courtesy of Arkansas Travelers

Arkansas Travelers at Dickey-Stephens Park

Hodgepodge Fun

Tickets:
Age 0-2: Free
Outfield Lawn: Age 3-17: $4.00; Age 18+: $6.00
Reserved: Age 3-7: $5.00; Age 18+: $8.00
Box: $12.00 per person

Parking:
Paid parking lots.

Parking:
No outside food or drink allowed.

400 West Broadway Street
North Little Rock, 72114
(501) 664 - 1555
http://www.milb.com/index.jsp?sid=t574

What to expect...

Dickey-Stephens Park is home to the Arkansas Travelers. The environment at Traveler's games is one of pure excitement. The air is filled with shouts from the vendors, smells of the famous foot-long corndogs, and the cheers of enthusiastic fans.

The ballpark is very clean and spacious. It is stroller-accessible, and offers an even a less-expensive option of sitting on the outfield lawn instead of purchasing seats. Often, families enjoy this choice because it allows children to run around. Several concession stands are located throughout the ballpark, making it very easy to grab a drink, a snack, or dinner for the whole family.

Attending a Travelers game is a traditional, sporting way to spend an evening. The backdrop for the baseball field is the Little Rock skyline and the downtown buildings. The Arkansas River sits right behind the ballpark. The scenery is beautiful, but make sure that you keep an eye out for any pop flies!

Just Around the Corner...

Old State House Museum

Riverfront Park

Robinson Center Music Hall

Eureka Springs & North Arkansas Railway

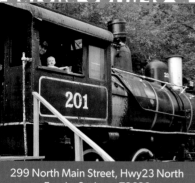

Hours:
The departures for the Excursion Train are Tuesday through Saturday at 10:30 AM, 12:00 PM, 2:30 PM, and an additional train ride at 4:00 PM on Saturdays. The Railway is open April through October, with Sunday trains on Memorial Day and Labor Day weekends.

Admission:
Age 0-3: Free; Age 4-10: $6.75; Age 11+: $13.50

Parking:
Free parking lot.

Food:
You may bring your own food and drink. Snacks and refreshments may be purchased at the Snack Car.

299 North Main Street, Hwy23 North
Eureka Springs, 72632
(479) 253-9623
www.esnarailway.com

What to expect...

Take a step back in time as you walk up to the counter at the Eureka Springs Depot to purchase train tickets. The train yard is filled with remnants of a previous era—vintage trains, boxcars, and automobiles are scattered about for kids to play on. Children are practically bouncing up and down to get on the train and there is nothing holding them back as the conductor checks his pocket watch, tips his hat, and leans out of the train to shout, "All aboard!"

The locomotive is from the 1940s, so the interior is spacious, allowing children to run up and down the aisle and pick whichever seat they like. The conductor walks around punching tickets and the nostalgia of traveling through the forest and over streams is nearly tangible. The windows can be opened to unleash a refreshing breeze and the seats can be adjusted to face forwards or backwards. The approximately 50-minute train ride is a picturesque, enjoyable four-and-a-half mile ride through the Ozark woodlands.

Halfway through the ride, the train comes to an abrupt halt and passengers can dig in their pockets for coins, follow the conductor outside, and watch as the train's engine slowly comes by and flattens the coins. There is also the opportunity to watch the engine get turned around on a turntable.

The Eureka Springs train provides an environment where children can run around, be loud, and learn about locomotives. This attraction is a must-do if you're vacationing in Eureka Springs or in a town nearby. It's well worth the drive!

There are no changing tables in the restrooms.

Hot Springs National Park

Hours:

The park is open year-round.

The visitor center in the Fordyce Bathhouse and the Bathhouse Row Emporium is open daily, 9:00 AM - 5:00 PM.

Parking:

Free and metered parking downtown is available along the streets. Parking lots are also available.

The visitor center is located downtown on Highway 7 or Central Avenue.
(501) 620 - 6715
www.nps.gov/hosp

What to expect...

Although Hot Springs offers beautiful, scenic drives, and miles of trails, my favorite part of the national park doesn't require a water bottle or hiking boots. What I love most is the bustling downtown with old, picturesque storefronts, bathhouses, and springs where locals fill up jugs of water from spigots on the road.

Hot Springs is a great day or weekend destination. Make sure that you pack a stroller if your little ones don't want to walk as much as Mom or Dad. The stores are adorable; you'd be remiss not to poke your head into several. With toy stores, restaurants, and taffy/fudge/ice cream parlors, I promise you'll discover at least a few shops that will make your children happy!

The city of Hot Springs offers many fun things to do. You should call or stop by the visitor center to get more information about activities going on during the year. A great way to end your day is at the Hot Springs Mountain Tower. The tower is located atop Hot Springs Mountain within the national park and affords a breathtaking view of the city and the Ouachita Mountains.

Movies in the Park

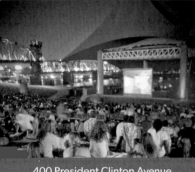

Hours:
Movies in the Park shows approximately eight movies on Wednesday evenings during the summer. The park opens at 6:30 PM. Check the website for dates and movies.

Admission:
FREE!

Parking:
Parking in the River Market District.

Food:
You may bring your own food and drink.

400 President Clinton Avenue
Little Rock, 72201
(501) 375 - 2552
http://moviesintheparklr.net

What to expect...

Movies in the Park is a great way to spend a summer evening—the Arkansas River in the background, a family-friendly movie playing, and time to relax and unwind. You can either sit in the dedicated seating up front or you can bring a blanket or lawn chair and sit on the grass. I prefer this, because you can lie down and the children have a little more room to roam.

Make sure that you bring bug spray! Because the amphitheater is located beside the Arkansas River, mosquitoes are often a problem. You may bring your own food and drinks—just no glass bottles. The concession stand offers drinks, popcorn, ice cream, and candy.

Make sure that you check the movie schedule. Movies in the Park does a good job of offering a wide variety of movies—from kid movies to family-friendly movies to date-night-only movies. They usually play at least two films per summer that are geared specifically for children.

You'll be glad that you brought your family to enjoy Movies in the Park.

Just Around the Corner...

Museum of Discovery

Peabody Park

River Rail

River Market District

What to expect...

Located on the South Shore of the Arkansas River, the River Market District is the heart and soul of downtown's entertainment district. With fun places to shop, amazing restaurants, and engaging museums around every corner, this is the perfect place to spend the day with your children. The River Market District has parks, libraries, two open pavilions, walkways all along the Arkansas River, museums, restaurants, beautiful hotels, gardens, and anything that is quintessentially Little Rock.

It's a good idea to pack a stroller (an easily-foldable umbrella stroller) and cash. You'll probably have to pay for parking in the metered parking lots/garages, unless you visit early on a Saturday morning. You will most definitely need cash to pay for some things, like the River Rail.

One of my favorite downtown activities is ice skating during the holiday season. You can check out the full calendar of concerts, festivals, and other special events taking place online.

For more information, you can visit the website at _www.rivermarket.info_ or call them at (501) 376 - 4781.

River Rail

Hours:
8:30 AM - 10:00 PM, Monday - Wednesday
8:30 AM - 12:00 AM, Thursday - Saturday
11:00 AM - 5:00 PM, Sunday

Admission:
Age 0-4: Free; Age 5-11: $0.50; Age 12-64: $1.00; Age 65+: $0.50

Parking:
Parking available in River Market District.

Food:
No outside food or drink allowed.

(501) 374 - 5354
www.cat.org/rrail/

What to expect...

The River Rail Electric Streetcar is a fun and inexpensive way to explore downtown Little Rock with your little ones. The bright yellow and red streetcars with spacious, wooden interiors and large windows make their way through the maze of downtown streets.

Make sure that you have exact change before boarding the River Rail. A day pass is $2.00, a three-day pass is $5.00, and a 20-ride card costs $15.00. Signs, located at each stopping point, make it easy to know where to wait. These 15 stops are the only places to hop on or off the River Rail: Main at 5th, Main at 7th, Maple at 6th, Maple at Broadway, Verizon Plaza Stop 120 at Main Street, Main Street Bridge Stop, President Clinton Ave. at River Market Ave., River Market Ave. at 3rd, Presidential Library/ Heifer International World Ave. at 3rd, 3rd at River Market Ave., Main Library Stop 2nd at Rock, Historic Arkansas Museum Stop 2nd at Scott, 2nd at Center, West Markham at Spring, and The Peabody Little Rock Stop Markham at Scott.

The Blue Line and the Green Line are the two different lines on the River Rail. The Green Line travels in Little Rock only and does not travel across the Main Street Bridge. The Blue Line travels the entire 3.4 mile route, providing service to all Little Rock and North Little Rock stops. The average loop time is 35 minutes for the Blue Line and 20 minutes for the Green Line.

Feeling Festive

Festivals provide a great opportunity to create family traditions. Although this chapter contains just a fraction of the festivals that take place around the state, these are my favorites—the ones I frequent with my children. I've attended the Greek Food Festival since I was a little girl, and now I take my children every year!

Courtesy of Emily Benton Ryan

Arkansas State Fair

2600 Howard Street
Little Rock, 72206
(501) 372-8341
www.arkansasstatefair.com

Hours:
Open daily at 11:00 AM. Runs in mid-October.
Admission:
Age 0-5: Free; Age 6-12: $4.00; Age 13-59: $8.00; Age 60+: $4.00
Parking:
Parking is $5.00. Cash only.
Food:
No outside food or drink allowed. Concession stands around the fair only accept cash. Picnic tables and benches are available but scarce, so be prepared to eat on your feet.
Discounts:
Monday - Friday from 11:00 AM - 1:00 PM, admission and parking are free. There are two days each year that are free for moms and kids. For additional discounts, check the fair's website.

What to expect...

Sounds of laughter, balloons bursting, vendors shouting, people shrieking on roller coasters, and music fill the air at the Arkansas State Fair where having fun is a guarantee for all ages. The fair holds the promise that fall has indeed arrived, and we can all celebrate by eating fried Oreos and admiring the beautiful view from the Ferris wheel.

Exciting rides abound. Family Land is dedicated to younger children (at least two years of age to ride without an adult), and there are plenty of rides that parents and children can embark on together. Your children will undoubtedly want to try their hand at popping balloons, shooting water guns, and swishing hoops in order to win an enormous stuffed animal. The most popular destinations for kids are the various petting zoos located throughout the fair. Remember to pack some hand sanitizer!

The Arkansas State Fair has a concert stage where performers put on shows for big crowds. The livestock pageants are also popular, showcasing horses, pigs, goats, and sheep.

Of course, a trip to the fair would not be complete without sampling some food. I don't even want to know how many calories I consume, but the fair only comes once a year, right!? My favorites are the corndogs, cotton candy, fried Oreos, and frozen lemonade.

The food vendors accept cash and the rides accept tickets which cost a dollar. Ticket booths are spread throughout the fair. Most of the rides cost no more than one or two tickets per person. Paths are wide and stroller-friendly. The best time to avoid the crowds is when the fair opens for the day. If you get there early, it's easy to get a close-in parking spot. Restrooms are located all over the fair, with changing tables in the women's restrooms.

Just Around the Corner...

Arkansas State Capitol

Little Rock Central High School National Historic Site

The Painted Pig

Greek Food Festival

Annunciation Greek Orthodox Church
1100 Napa Valley Drive
Little Rock, 72211
(501) 221 - 5300
www.greekfoodfest.com

Hours: Usually the third weekend in May
11:00 AM - 9:00 PM, Friday and Saturday
12:00 PM - 6:00 PM, Sunday

Admission:
FREE!

Parking:
Free parking is available along Napa Valley Drive. Two trolleys run every ten minutes from Asbury United Methodist Church (1700 Napa Valley Drive) and Pulaski Academy (12601 Hinson Road).

Food:
You may bring your own food and drink though the festival offers a mouth-watering array of Greek foods and desserts. Plenty of benches, tables, chairs, and open areas are available for you to enjoy the nice weather and yummy food.

What to expect...

There are few things for which I can say, "I've never missed it," but for the Greek Food Festival, it's the truth! I've never missed it! I looked forward to it all year when I was younger. If you attend, I can promise that between the wonderful entertainment (Greek music, Greek dancing, etc.) and the mouth-watering food, you won't ever miss this festival.

A great way to enjoy the Greek Food Festival is to come for lunch. I delight in watching the dances, with the beautiful, authentic music and dancers dressed in Greek outfits. You can sit down and watch the entertainment while dining on Greek food (the gyros, Greek salad, and baklava are my personal favorites!). In case you have a picky eater on your hands, hotdogs are also sold.

The Greek Food Festival is the largest ethnic festival in the state, so be prepared for big crowds and a distant parking space. Unless you plan on riding the trolley, bring a stroller for the little ones. If you're just interested in dining on the Greek cuisine, the festival offers a drive-thru. Don't be scared: the line always looks long, but the cars get through quickly. Only cash is accepted.

Tours are offered of the beautiful interior of the church. Within it are stands of intricate Greek crafts and trinkets, as well as tables of Greek pastries.

The Kids' Center has a climbing wall and bouncy houses. There are rides, face painting, crafts, a candy walk, and plenty of stuff for children to enjoy!

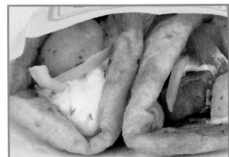

Harvest Festival

Hours:
10:00 AM - 6:00 PM, Saturday
12:00 PM - 6:00 PM, Sunday
Mid-October

Admission:
Age 0-5: Free; Age 6-12: $5.00; Age 13+: $10.00

Parking:
Free parking lot.

Food:
No outside food or drink allowed. There are a couple of concession stands that offer snacks and refreshments.

Wildwood Park for the Arts
20919 Denny Road
Little Rock, 72223
(501) 821-7275
www.wildwoodpark.org

What to expect...

Harvest Festival at Wildwood Park offers an abundance of activities, sights, and sounds for the entire family. Situated around Swan Lake and surrounded by woods, the festival promises a day of strolling along the miles of paths, exploring the hay fort and pumpkin patch, engaging in crafts such as pumpkin painting, and going on an adventurous hayride.

Sounds of bluegrass music from the Arkansas Pickin' and Fiddlin' Championship fill the air as you walk around the festival. You may also sit on the spacious lawn and watch the dueling musicians. The element of folk music gives rise to nostalgic feelings of the beauty of autumn in Arkansas.

For the little ones, there are crafts tables, sack races, hay bale mazes, a hay ride, and ample space to run around. My son's favorite attraction was the model train exhibit. In the south lobby and south lawn of the Cabe Festival Theatre, train enthusiasts display their trains. Inside are detailed trains, and children can watch as they circle past mountains, around skyscrapers, and under tunnels.

Most of the park is paved, so a stroller would do fine. Make sure that you bring cash, because many of the attractions cost extra and you will need to purchase "wild bucks" for the activities.

Just Around the Corner...

Arkansas Skatium Ice Rink

Arkansas Skatium Roller Rink

Pinnacle Mountain State Park

Jewish Food Festival

400 President Clinton Avenue
Little Rock, 72201
(501) 663 - 3571
www.jewisharkansas.org

Hours:
10:00 AM - 4:00 PM, typically on the last Sunday in April
or the first Sunday in May

Admission:
FREE!

Parking:
Parking in the River Market District.

Food:
You may bring your own food and drink. Picnic tables
and benches are available.

What to expect...

Similar to the Greek Food Festival, the Jewish Food Festival
is a wonderful way to learn about the culture, religion
and Jewish holidays, while enjoying amazing food and
entertainment. The festival is located in the River Market
Pavilion, so the shade coupled with the breezes from the
Arkansas River make this an ideal location.

In 2012, over 12,000 people came to enjoy the festival and
sample the delectable cuisine from kabobs to falafel and
Israeli salad. A children's play area with face painting and a
jumping house is quite popular. The entertainment includes
traditional and contemporary Jewish music that fills the
pavilion and adds a rich aspect to the festival.

Since the festival is located under and around the pavilion,
you can bring a stroller. Whenever we go, we enjoy eating
our lunch behind the pavilion and taking in the gorgeous
views of the Arkansas River and Riverfront Park. Your children
will be fascinated with learning about Jewish culture,
customs, and foods. It's a great way to expand their horizons!

Riverfest

Hours:

6:00 PM - 11:00 PM, Friday
11:00 AM - 11:00 PM, Saturday
1:00 PM - 11:00 PM, Sunday

Riverfest is usually the last weekend in May. Check the website for exact dates.

Admission:

Age 0-6: Free; Tickets bought in advance: $20.00; 3-day Pass: $30.00.

Tickets may be purchased at the gate with cash only.

Parking:

Parking in the River Market District.

Food:

No outside food or drink allowed.

500 President Clinton Avenue
Little Rock, 72201
(501) 225 - 3378
http://riverfestarkansas.com

What to expect...

Along the banks of the Arkansas River, Riverfest offers fun entertainment, education, and activities geared solely for younger ones. From face painting and bouncy houses, to fire safety and gymnastic performances, your children are sure to have a great time and be very entertained. The food at Riverfest will make them happy as well. Who can complain about cotton candy, corndogs, and caramel apples?

When attending Riverfest with little ones, the trick is to arrive early. Parking can be challenging, so arrive early. On another note, the evening activities and performances are not appropriate for children.

The Riverfest website is exceptional; definitely take the time to check it out before heading to the festival. If you do have to park farther away, the River Rail is open during all hours of Riverfest. Just find a River Rail location, and park close to that.

Wye Mountain Daffodil Festival

22300 Highway 113
Bigelow, 72016
(501) 330 - 2403

Hours:
9:00 AM - 5:00 PM, daily in early to mid-March.

Admission:
FREE!

Parking:
Free parking lot.

Food:
You may bring your own food and drink. A concession stand is located by the entrance.

What to expect...

Nothing says Arkansas to me quite like the Wye Mountain Daffodil Festival (okay, maybe second to the Arkansas Razorbacks) where people from all over the state gather to buy flowers, enjoy the scenery, and take family pictures. It celebrates the welcoming of spring, and nothing could be more beautiful than the open field of daffodils gracing the hillside next to the small United Methodist Church that sponsors the event.

Children can run around the flowers that have no rhyme or reason to their placement. While it might not be the most exciting festival in the state, you will be glad you brought your children to experience it. A small shop offers crafts for sale, and you can also purchase daffodils and bulbs. All of the proceeds go to the church's minister.

The field is open daily, but the festival takes place on Saturday and Sunday. While you can bring strollers, you cannot bring pets. Pack a picnic lunch and enjoy the one-of-a-kind beauty of being surrounded by an endless ocean of bright yellow and white daffodils.

The festival has no official website, but you can find it on Facebook under "Wye Mountain Daffodil Festival."

Courtesy of Emily Benton Ryan

Photo Credits

All photos listed start from the top left corner of each page, then follow clockwise. All unlabeled photos are taken by Emily Benton Ryan or are part of the Ryan collection.

3: Photo courtesy of somerlynne.com

8: Photo courtesy of Bill Benton

11: Photos courtesy of Arkansas Arts Center

12: Photos courtesy of Arkansas Arts Center

13: Photos courtesy of Little Rock Convention and Visitors Bureau

14: Photos courtesy of Little Rock Convention and Visitors Bureau

15: Photo courtesy of Historic Arkansas Museum ; Photo courtesy of Little Rock Convention and Visitors Bureau

17: Photo courtesy of Central High Museum Historical Collections ; Photo courtesy Ben Wagner

18: Photo courtesy of Little Rock Convention and Visitors Bureau; Photo courtesy MacArthur Museum of Military History

19: Photos courtesy of Emily Benton Ryan

20: Photo courtesy of Little Rock Convention and Visitors Bureau; Photo courtesy Emily Benton Ryan

21: Photos courtesy of Museum of Discovery

22: Photo courtesy of Emily Benton Ryan

23: Photos courtesy of Emily Benton Ryan

24: Photos courtesy of Little Rock Convention and Visitors Bureau

25: Photos courtesy of Children's Theatre

26: Photos courtesy of Little Rock Convention and Visitors Bureau

27: Photos courtesy of Murry's Dinner Playhouse

22: Photo courtesy of Children's Theatre

29: Photos courtesy of Children's Theatre

30: Photos courtesy of Little Rock Convention and Visitors Bureau

31: Photos courtesy of Firefly

32: Photos courtesy of All Aboard Restaurant and Grill

33: Photo courtesy of Altitude Trampoline Park

34: Photos courtesy of Altitude Trampoline Park

35: Photos courtesy of Scott Ryan

36: Photos courtesy of Scott Ryan

37: Photo courtesy of Emily Benton Ryan ; Photos courtesy of Scott Ryan

38: Photos courtesy of Tasha Young

39: Photo courtesy of Little Rock Convention and Visitors Bureau; Photo courtesy of Little Rock Climbing Center

40: Photo courtesy of Millennium Bowl

41: Photos courtesy of The Painted Pig

42: Photos courtesy of Emily Benton Ryan

43: Photo courtesy of Emily Benton Ryan

44: Photo courtesy of Rock Creek; Photo courtesy of Fawn Rechkemmer (www. insteadofthedishes.com)

45: Photos courtesy of Scott Ryan

45: Photos courtesy of The Wonder Place

47: Photo courtesy of Emily Benton Ryan

48: Photo courtesy of Emily Benton Ryan

49: Photo courtesy of Sonia Knapp

50: Photo courtesy of Central Arkansas Library System

51: Photo courtesy of Emily Benton Ryan

52: Photos courtesy of Emily Benton Ryan

53: Photos courtesy of Magic Springs

54: Photo courtesy of Emily Benton Ryan; Photos courtesy of Little Rock Convention and Visitors Bureau; Photo courtesy of Emily Benton Ryan

55: Photos courtesy of Emily Benton Ryan

56: Photos courtesy of Wild River Country

57: Photo courtesy of Emily Benton Ryan

58: Photos courtesy of Emily Benton Ryan

59: Photo courtesy of Little Rock Convention and Visitors Bureau; Photo courtesy of Todd Mikel Smith

Photo Credits

60/61: Photos courtesy of Blanchard Springs Caverns

62: Photos courtesy of Emily Benton Ryan

63: Photos courtesy of Arkansas State Parks

64: Photo courtesy of Emily Benton Ryan; Photo courtesy of Stock.xchng.com

65: Photos courtesy of Emily Benton Ryan

66: Photo courtesy of Emily Benton Ryan

67: Photo courtesy of Emily Benton Ryan; 66: Photo courtesy of Mt. Magazine State Park; Photo courtesy of Emily Benton Ryan

68: Photos courtesy of Emily Benton Ryan

69: Photo courtesy of Little Rock Convention and Visitors Bureau; Photo courtesy of Emily Benton Ryan

70/71: Photos courtesy of Emily Benton Ryan

72: Photo courtesy of Little Rock Convention and Visitors Bureau; Photo courtesy of Emily Benton Ryan

73: Photos courtesy of Little Rock Convention and Visitors Bureau

74: Photos courtesy of Arkansas State Parks

75: Photo courtesy of Todd Mikel Smith; Photo courtesy of stockxchng.com

75: Photo courtesy of Little Rock Convention and Visitors Bureau; Photo courtesy of stockxchng.com

77: Photo courtesy of Emily Benton Ryan

78: Photo courtesy of Christi Fisher; Photo courtesy of Gretchen Davis; Photo courtesy of Leanna Conine

79: Photo courtesy of Evie Scherrey

80: Photo courtesy of Emily Benton Ryan

81: Photo courtesy of Little Rock Convention and Visitors Bureau

82: Photos courtesy of Emily Benton Ryan

83: Photos courtesy of Emily Benton Ryan

84: Photo courtesy of ACH; Photo courtesy of Arkansas State Park; Photo courtesy of ACH

85: Photo courtesy of Emily Benton Ryan; Photo courtesy of stock.xchng.com

86: Photo courtesy of Emily Benton Ryan; Photo courtesy of stock.xchng.com

87: Photo courtesy of Little Rock Zoo

88: Photos courtesy of Little Rock Zoo

89: Photos courtesy of Little Rock Zoo

90: Photos courtesy of Emily Benton Ryan

91: Photo courtesy of Arkansas Travelers

92: Photos courtesy of Arkansas Travelers

93: Photos courtesy of Emily Benton Ryan

94: Photos courtesy of Emily Benton Ryan

95: Photos courtesy of Little Rock Convention and Visitors Bureau

96: Photos courtesy of Little Rock Convention and Visitors Bureau

97: Photos courtesy of Emily Benton Ryan

98: Photo courtesy of Little Rock Convention and Visitors Bureau; Photo courtesy of Emily Benton Ryan; Photo courtesy of Christi Fisher

99: Photo courtesy of Emily Benton Ryan

100: Photos courtesy of Emily Benton Ryan

101: Photo courtesy of Emily Benton Ryan; Photo courtesy of Little Rock Convention and Visitors Bureau; Photo courtesy of Emily Benton Ryan

102: Photos courtesy of Annunciation GreekOrthodox Church; Photo courtesy of stock.xchng.com

103: Photos courtesy of Emily Benton Ryan

104: Photo courtesy of stock.xchng.com; Photo courtesy of Emily Benton Ryan; Photo courtesy of stock.xchng.com

105: Photo courtesy of Little Rock Convention and Visitors Bureau; Photo courtesy of stock.xchng.com

106: Photos courtesy of Emily Benton Ryan

107: Photos courtesy of Emily Benton Ryan

128: Photo courtesy of Marci Burns

Index

Index

Alphabetical Site Index

Notes

Notes

Notes

Notes

Notes

Notes

Notes

Notes

Notes

Notes

Notes

Notes

Notes

Notes

Notes

Notes

About the Author

Emily Benton Ryan grew up in Little Rock. She graduated with a Bachelor's degree in English from Baylor University and a Master's degree in Professional Writing from the University of Arkansas at Little Rock.

Before having children, Emily enjoyed writing poetry, taking naps, and being organized. And now, you can keep up with her crazy life through her blog, "Hush Puppies, Gumbo, and Fried Green Tomatoes: The Culinary, Gardening, Wordjibberishness, and Familial Adventures of a Blonde, Southern Gal," at www. emssouthernliving.blogspot.com.